THE F WORD

Lily Pebbles

HODDER &
STOUGHTON

First published in Great Britain in 2018 by Hodder & Stoughton
An Hachette UK company

6

Copyright © Lily Pebbles 2018

The right of Lily Pebbles to be identified as the Author of the Work has been
asserted by her in accordance with the Copyright, Designs and Patents Act 1988.

This book is a work of non-fiction based on the life, experiences and
recollections of the author. In some cases names of people, places and
certain details have been changed to protect the privacy of others.

A CIP catalogue record for this title is available from the British Library

Hardback ISBN 9781473680166
Trade Paperback ISBN 9781473680173
eBook ISBN 9781473680180

Typeset in Celeste by Hewer Text UK Ltd, Edinburgh
Printed and bound by Clays Ltd, St Ives plc

Hodder & Stoughton policy is to use papers that are natural, renewable
and recyclable products and made from wood grown in sustainable
forests. The logging and manufacturing processes are expected to
conform to the environmental regulations of the country of origin.

Hodder & Stoughton Ltd
Carmelite House
50 Victoria Embankment
London EC4Y 0DZ

www.hodder.co.uk

For all the incredible women in my life . . .
Especially my beautiful grandma, Teresa.

INTRODUCTION

Not too long ago, I was curled up on my friend's sofa with a cup of tea catching up on work, wedding caterers and pregnant friends. A pretty normal set-up for us really; we're not big on phone calls. Well, I'm not big on phone calls; spontaneous tea chats are my thing! Despite my obvious attempt to avoid a conversation I was worried she wanted to broach, she blurted out: 'I think we're going to move to Australia for a few years.' And there it was. That old but not forgotten feeling when your first real boyfriend says, 'We need to talk.' The lump in your throat and pressure in your eyes that warns you if you even attempt to talk, you're going to burst into tears and not be able to stop. I of course did the whole supportive friend thing, whilst (not so) secretly hoping that the plan would completely fall through and never become a reality. Because if it did, it would be so much worse than a teenage break-up. It would mean putting a 10,000-mile-long speed bump in the middle of a perfectly great 30-year-long love story. It would mean no more spontaneous tea chats but occasional early morning scheduled FaceTime calls instead. It was heartbreaking, and the only person I wanted to talk to about it, the only person who would comfort me in the right way and make sense of all my irrational thoughts, was the person sitting next to me pissing off to Australia!

Girlfriends, eh? It's never straightforward.

If my 1998 diary is anything to go by, female friend-ships are incredibly complex and emotional. I often go back and read it, partly because my eleven-year-old self is so dramatic and hilarious, but mainly because it reminds me how lucky I am to have such long-standing friendships. I kept a diary on and off from the age of ten to 16, updating it each year as I'd reinvent my handwriting style. I don't remember anyone ever encouraging me to do so but I was obsessed with stationery growing up, and after spending a few months writing down everything I saw, pretending to be 'Harriet the Spy', I decided to use my notebooks for something more personal. I didn't write in it every day but when I remembered, in the

evenings, I'd sit up in bed and start 'Dear Diary', signing off 'See ya later, Lil x', sometimes even asking
'How are you? I'm fine'. It was my private time, I
couldn't pass or fail; all I had to do was write down
what I had been up to and how I was feeling and no
one would ever read it. I went to town, *really* over-
sharing on the details at times; let's just say it's unfor-
tunate that it coincided with a lot of 'firsts'. I'd say
70% of the contents is far too embarrassing to ever
show anyone, but 30% is pure gold and I've been
known in the past to perform readings to my friends
over a takeaway. It was so long ago that even the
bitchiest of diary entries has us howling with laughter – I'd even say that showing such honesty actually
brings us closer together. My childhood friendships
are so precious to me and over time I've had to nurture
those relationships into adult life. As a result, they've
changed over the years – and at times they've been
challenged. I often reflect on the incredible women
I've met along the course of my journey and how
these relationships have completely shaped my life.
Unlike family, you pick your friends and I'm lucky to
have friends I've known for over 25 years, but I've
also made new ones as an adult and the dynamics and
intricacies of these relationships is a whole new story.

It remains true though that in my life, almost every decision, experience and memory comes with a female companion somewhere behind the scenes. At 30 years old I feel confident in knowing that I am a good friend, but it's without a doubt my female friends who've taught me how to be one. I think if I wasn't they wouldn't have stuck around for so long and in our 'old age' we've all begun speaking more honestly about friendship, acknowledging what we've got and gushing to each other about the importance we hold in each other's lives. We should never take for granted the importance of female friendships; they can affect everything we do, can feed into all aspects of our lives and they've helped me learn so much about myself along the way.

It always saddens me that the media encourages women to compare themselves to each other and as a result we're often putting ourselves up against one another. We're expected to be in competition and the phenomenal success of films like *Mean Girls* and the more recent *Bridesmaids* is evidence that a lot of women relate to this so-called 'bitchiness' and the pressure to fit in and keep up with other women. But I refuse to believe that's how it should be, and I want to write a book that celebrates the relationships women

have. This book is going to be about female friendships, and all the strings attached!

Our friendships with other women are so intricate
and complex, they're something we invest time in and
work hard to maintain. Some feel completely easy, no
effort needed, but I think we all know how it feels to
have to work a little harder on others. Every single
friendship we have is unique and no two friendships
are the same, but perhaps we look to them all for the
same things: companionship, trust, support, and for
someone to be able to make you laugh when all you
can think to do is cry!

For some women, it's holding onto friends that's
hard, for others it's letting go. Acknowledging and
moving on from a toxic friendship is no different from
ending a romantic relationship; uncertainty and fear
must be pushed aside in place of a gut feeling and a
need to be selfish. Growing up, it was all a numbers
game: the more friends you had, the more popular you
were, but as adults we reach a turning point where
suddenly it's just those few important friendships that
matter. Quality supersedes quantity.

The thing to remember is that you're never too old
to make a new friend. They say making a new friend
is like falling in love and scientists have recently found

that the hormones released in the brain when two women meet and go on to form a friendship are the same as those found in the brain when you fall for someone romantically. And I'm not surprised; friendship at first sight is something many of us will have experienced, a moment of undeniable friend chemistry. Perhaps you're the only two people who laugh at a comment made in a meeting, or you openly share a truth about yourself only to hear someone utter the words: 'Oh my God, me too!' There's a spark. A flash of recognition. A mutual understanding. And suddenly you feel less alone.

Perhaps it's also true that we cross paths with certain women when we need to, at specific points in our lives. And then sometimes those paths head in different directions and the friendship, having done its job, dissipates. Growing apart emotionally is just life doing its thing and although it's sad, I believe everything happens for a reason. When physical distance comes between friends it's hard to keep hold of what was there and it almost feels unfair, as if you're waiting for life to shift and get things back into order. But perhaps there's something to be said for giving friendships some room and space to breathe. Sometimes there is a whole new closeness that can be found in distance.

When you read this book, I want the stories and the observations to make you feel appreciative of your friendships no matter how complicated they are. You might have one or two female friends or a whole group of them. Or you might feel like you have no real friendships with women, but maybe you're just not noticing what's right there in front of you and the important relationships that have shaped you as a person. Maybe it'll give you the confidence to go out and meet other women who are also looking to make new friends. I would *really* love that, and I hope you can feel enlightened by the women in your life and the roles that they play. I don't think there is a norm and there are no rules when it comes to female friendships. I hope this book makes you realise how lucky you are to be surrounded by such challenging, beautiful, demanding, kind, ridiculous, aspirational, difficult and amazing women. I know that writing it has made me feel just that.

PLAYGROUNDS, PARTIES & PLASTERS

Let's take a trip down memory lane to where it all began, because for me the root of all my friendships comes from those made at a very young age. In my opinion, early-childhood friendship is rarely given enough credit for the impact it can have on your life; for some people those early days might just be a distant memory but they're the beginning of my story and the reason why my female friendships mean so much to me.

I was encouraged to be a sociable kid from day one with two older friends pretty much waiting on standby for me to be born. Jake, my mum's best friend's son, is 19 months older than me; we were inseparable growing up and two years ago he officiated my wedding. Hannah was born a year before me and lived right next door; still to this day she tells people that my mum decided to have a third child because of how cute she was. To be fair, my sisters are seven and ten years older than me and I don't think my mum was planning on having any more kids, so the story matches up and, well, she *was* very cute. My family has always given her the nickname 'Happy Hannah' because of her infectious energy that perfectly suited her wild curly hair.

My earliest memory with Hannah is having her at my third birthday party, lighting up the room as always, dressed in a floral party dress, but we became really inseparable friends (without our mums' encouragement) from around five. Being the younger one I was in awe of everything she did growing up. I'd copy what she wore, mimic the way she spoke; and to me she was the most confident, brave and kind person I knew. I always joke that Hannah taught me how to talk because until the age of 15 I was painfully shy around people I didn't know and by watching and spending time with her I learnt how to socialise and be less awkward around new people. In our teenage years, she'd always invite me to her house parties despite the fact I'd stand in the corner in silence, but I remember she'd always make the effort to introduce me to her friends and encourage me to get involved.

In those first few years Hannah and Jake were my friendship group, but it was at three years old at nursery that I chose my first friend myself.

I think as you get older you consider your friendships more and almost judge a new friend on what they can bring to your life, but when you're three years old it's a completely natural instinct that draws you to someone. Maybe it was the hairband they wore or their contagious laugh; maybe they shared a toy with you or complimented you on your new shoes. For me it was simple: Debs and I bonded over a shared love of cheating the nursery system. We volunteered ourselves for the roles of milk and cookie monitors, and quickly developed a plan that would involve grabbing an extra cookie for ourselves on most days. We also managed to work the sandpit system, making sure we bypassed the rota and always went in together. So, we were basically thieving, lying kids ... *it was instant love.* I don't remember our very first meeting, but when I watch back old videos of our Easter nursery show it's clear from the grip of our tiny holding hands that we had no interest in anyone else but each other. We quickly became more than just nursery friends, convincing our mums to let us spend time together out of hours. Every Friday we'd all go for lunch, which is when I first learnt of Debs' painfully fussy eating, waiting an extra 20 minutes for a hamburger with absolutely nothing but the burger inside the bun. I found it so funny and strange but I embraced our differences, sometimes ordering for her, showing off that I knew what she liked. We started ballet lessons together; I chose to wear baby pink whereas Debs opted for an all-black outfit, stylish from day one, and of course we only ever wanted to be paired together.

At three years old, all you really need is one buddy, someone to have your back and enjoy the same things you do. But with school comes a whole new social rule book and making friends can be incredibly scary. After nursery, because we didn't live in the same area, Debs and I went to different schools and according to my mum neither of us were happy about it at all. But our mums got on well so we stayed in touch, seeing each other on weekends and always inviting each other to our birthday parties. I'll never forget Debs turning up to my fifth birthday dressed as Batman when all the other girls wore their prettiest party dresses; I think her refusal to conform is what I loved and still love most about her.

Growing up I thought it was normal to have an 'out-of-school best friend' but now looking back I am amazed that we stayed so close despite never going to school together after nursery. I felt like Debs was a reflection of my friendship achievements and I loved introducing her to my school friends, showing her off and thinking, *Look who I met before I even started school.* My school friends would have met Debs at my fifth and sixth birthday parties but it was probably from around seven years old that they all really started to mix. She was very shy at first, having to spend time with a group of kids she didn't know, but I remember really making the effort to integrate her into the group. I'd often host sleepovers in my living room; some would sleep in sleeping bags on the sofas but most of us piled onto the 'duvet bed' my mum would make on the floor. She'd move the coffee table out and lay all the duvets we had in the house on top of each other, making the most comfortable giant bed on the floor for us all to share. I'd hand out cartons of Nesquik chocolate milk and Maryland chocolate chip cookies and we'd stay up late whispering and giggling. Although it was daunting for her, Debs would always come along and everyone got on really well; clearly I've always enjoyed introducing friends.

Those first years at school are where you learn how

to make friends without much guidance; you use what few skills you have to barter your way into partnerships and then build up your crew from there. We'd swap the contents of our packed lunches, share colouring pencils and if you were lucky and you had the right Pogs or Crazy Bones you had serious playground power. By Year One I'd sussed it all out and found my group of friends; honestly, I'm not sure how we all gravitated towards each other but before I knew it myself, Keisha, SJ and Jenny were calling ourselves a gang . . . and our gang was called 'Bad'. I mean, how my parents didn't see 18 years of disappointing school reports coming, I have no idea! We named ourselves 'Bad' because we thrived off being naughty and 'Bad' had one main mission: to get hold of as many plasters from the school nurse as possible. We'd do anything to succeed. According to my six-year-old self, a plaster was the most fun and cool accessory to have, so we'd purposely fall over on the gravel, fake-cry to the nurse and receive the treasure. Some members of the gang were naughtier than others; I was still a little shy at this point, but we all equally loved being together, being in a group and being silly. We came together instinctively and formed a team, and this small group of four became my first real friendship group, which just grew stronger and stronger throughout our school years.

I think one of the main reasons we all stayed so close was because of the relationships between our mums that bloomed out of our friendships. My mum would often pick me up from school and be greeted by an overexcited daughter begging to have her friends over after school or to go to theirs. It didn't take long for the mums to realise that they all got on really well too and our after-school hangouts became more regular. We'd run up to the bedroom to play Dreamphone whilst they sat downstairs and chatted over a cup of tea. I've always been inspired by how my mum treats her friends and I do think one of the best things you can do as a parent is encourage and nurture your child's friendships. Our mums took note of our friendships and always supported them; I remember SJ's mum would always add an extra Twix into her lunchbox for Jenny because she loved them. There is no doubt of the importance of these early friendships in encouraging higher self-esteem later in life and how helpful having a good support system of friends can be during tough times.

For me, the early days of school were also an opportunity to mix with people from all different backgrounds. Within our group of four we had a mix of backgrounds: SJ and I were English but with Jewish heritage, Jenny's family was Nigerian and Keisha's Guyanese. A story we always laugh about now is five-year-old Keisha asking her mum at dinner 'Am I Jewish?' and her mum replying 'No darling, you're not, why?' 'Because Lily keeps asking me if I am.' I'd probably just figured out that I was Jewish myself and assumed that meant everyone else was too! I loved going to Jenny's house; it was filled with beautiful bright fabrics and gold detailing like nothing I'd ever seen before, and at Keisha's house she used to show us little statues of the Hindu gods, explaining what they represented. We embraced our differences and enjoyed sharing them with each other.

Making friends at a young age is important but keeping them is definitely a struggle and at times it wasn't easy, but I appreciate those friends so much more because of how long we've stayed close and they've been a huge part of making me 'me'.

... *the one you've known forever*

THE CHILDHOOD FRIEND

The childhood friend knows all your stories; they've heard them a million times. They're aware of all the flaws in your personality and they accepted them a long time ago. The childhood friend loves to reminisce about the past but perhaps isn't the best person to discuss the future with. You can go months without seeing each other and when you do the chemistry is always still there. They don't really know what you do for work and you'd struggle to explain what they do to a stranger, but they can tell you exactly what your child-hood ambitions were. They effortlessly list your firsts, like your first kiss, your first job, your first heartbreak. It's almost mortifying the embarrassing moments and stories they remember from the awkward pre-teen days. When it comes to happiness, they're up there on the scale of cry-laughing, and you leave every meet-up looking forward to the next. There can be bumps in the road when changes occur, but the underlying love means you'll always learn to forgive and accept. This friendship can feel so easy but don't be tempted to take this underlying love for granted. As you start to branch off in different directions, taking the time to acknowledge your differences in a positive way will keep you close. Be consistent with checking in, keep them involved with what you're up to and never lose interest in what they're doing too.

Do: *Integrate your older childhood friendships in with your newer adult friendships to keep them current.*

Don't: *Become lazy with communication; even the older friendships deserve your time and attention.*

THE SPICE GIRLS ERA

I didn't really know what being a feminist meant until I was a teenager but in those early days, without realising it, we learnt together what feminism meant to us. I was born in 1987, which meant that in 1996, when The Spice Girls released 'Wannabe', I was nine and 'If you wanna be my lover, you gotta get with my friends' was something we took seriously. Friendship became a priority and Girl Power was real.

Having strong-minded female friends has always played a massive part in teaching me about equality and it gave me the confidence to stand my ground. If a boy teased me or tried to embarrass me in front of the class I knew that one of my girls would be there to support me as I stood up to him. Or if someone was talking about me behind my back, my friends would be there to tell them to stop and to comfort me. The group gave us confidence, maybe even too much at times. We'd run out to the playground at break time, gather our 'fans' (younger girls we'd force to watch us) and get into our starting positions on the steps leading up to the hall doors. With Keisha and I (the tall ones) at the back and Jenny and SJ at the front, 'Say You'll Be There' was usually our first choice of song and I spent most lunchtimes practising my high kick. As we moved from the infant to the junior school, we were split into different classes and I remember being sent the new class list during the summer holidays and feeling totally heartbroken. I couldn't imagine going to school and not sitting with my best friends every day. Keisha found out the news and cried her eyes out so the mums all decided to try and convince the school to keep us together. They went in for a meeting, fought for our friendship, told them we loved school because we were all together and they got us put back into the same class.

Being in a group meant we never felt intimidated, especially in the playground. There was a game the boys would play called 'The Ball Game', *creative name*, but the girls usually opted out and left them to it. One lunchtime we decided we were bored of playing 'Gunge Attack', a game we made up that basically consisted of balancing along the flower beds and not falling into the 'gunge'. We wanted to join in on The Ball Game, so we gathered some more friends and convinced the boys to let us join in. I could be quite timid at times so I remember feeling a bit scared of getting hit by the ball, but we did it as a team and whenever one of us got the ball we'd make sure we all got a turn to throw it. Joining in with a playground game was such a small thing but it felt so empowering at the time and it gave us all so much confidence.

Something I'll never forget is when my friends and I started the first girls' football team at school with the help of our dads and an encouraging Year Five teacher. SJ was always really into football, a passion that was passed down from her sisters, and our dads had become friends – conveniently they both supported the same Premiership team. There was always a boys' team but now that we had become confident in the school playground, we questioned why there wasn't one for the girls, too. Our teacher got permission from the headmistress and our dads clubbed together to sponsor us so that we could get a proper kit. We trained every Tuesday morning for an hour before school started; our kit was black-and-yellow stripes, we wore shin pads under knee-high socks and proper metal-studded boots so we looked like the real deal. We played like the real deal too! Thanks to our dads' Arsenal obsession they taught us to train like Premier League footballers, running back and forth on the pitch, jumping up and down and touching the ground, whilst they shouted instructions from the side line. And when it came to competing against other schools it completely freaked out the opposing team; in fact some of the other parents would complain, saying we were taking it too seriously. Looking back now it really makes me laugh; we hardly even celebrated goals because we 'had to' concentrate on the rest of the game.

Our mums would come to every match, too; Keisha's always brought orange slices in Tupperware to hand out during half-time. We all had our different role within the team; Keisha was our Tony Adams playing defence at the back, Jenny and SJ were feisty midfielders (our Ian Wright and Emmanuel Petit) and I used to play forward as the striker – I like to think I was the Thierry Henry but it's highly unlikely. Hannah, who was in the year above us at school, also joined the team so for me I made some of the best memories of my life, surrounded by best friends, having the time of our lives. We won medals and trophies competing against other schools and I still have them now, stashed away in my childhood memory box.

At the time, it was just fun to feel a part of a team and to have our own kit, but now I realise that it was our attitude of saying 'Why not?' when we were told 'No' that made us into strong young women. It also came in handy when we pushed for the girls to be able to wear trousers at school. My friend Keisha – who ironically later went on to become an international model – hated having her legs on show at school. We all had our insecurities but for Keisha she felt exposed by not being able to dress the way she wanted to. We turned her problem into *our* problem and our mums went to the headmistress with signatures from other parents to complain that we found it too cold and uncomfortable wearing skirts and that we wanted the option to wear trousers like the boys did. After our mums got the other parents on board and found the perfect trouser option to present to them, the school agreed to our request. Although it may not seem like a big deal now, that small win felt like a huge success against something we felt was unjust during a time when kids weren't that outspoken. It felt like winning a marathon and it reminded us that we had the power to make change happen if we really cared enough about something. It was never a question – if the boys could do something, so could we, and it was the strength of our female friendships that taught us that.

During our last two years of primary school the football team had brought us even closer together, but naturally as we had grown up, we'd developed more of our own personalities within the group. Certain traits that we'd never noticed before started to shine brighter and we were no longer all completely equal; now there was 'the one who aces all the tests', 'the one who makes us all laugh', 'the one who's the most beautiful' and 'the bossy one' (that was me). Before then we'd never really noticed who was cleverer than who, or who was getting more attention from the boys, and I think as our tween emotions kicked in it felt quite overwhelming not knowing how to deal with them. One day I came into school wearing the same zip-front Kickers shoes and C&A coat as Keisha; we used to always match, but that day she'd decided that she had grown up and wanted her *own* style. She was furious that I'd copied her and I was so embarrassed, but thankfully after a day of not talking to me something funny happened to distract her and we went back to being good friends. As a group, we were strong enough not to let any negative emotions damage our friendships on the surface, but I know personally I found myself sometimes feeling competitive or insecure, especially when it came to boys.

The Fab Four

A Fall oue

Lily Jenny keisha S-J

My homemade magazine (front cover)

A Fall Out
On the way
back home
from the
Isle of Wight
Lily and Jenny
had a fight.
Lily was being
really moody and
so she fell asleep
on the coach.
Lily had been
having a fight
with Sharukh.
When Lily was
in a deep sleep
Jenny tapped her
and woke her up.
She said that
Sharukh said sorry
but he didn't. Lily got

so mad steam
nearly came out
her ears and nose.

Fashion Fight
Keisha had
this really nice
coat. It had fake
fur round the neck
and it was water
proof. Lily asked her
if she could get it
and keisha said yes.
The next day Lily
came to school with
the coat on. Keisha
got mad and
said she said
Lily couldn't get it.
Lily thought keisha must
of forgotten.

My homemade magazine (Page 1)

I remember the first time I really fell for a boy. I was nine years old, and he was in the other class. I'd spend my evenings desperately thinking of something funny to say to him in the playground the following day, my heart would race every time he acknowledged my existence and just being around him would make me nervous. I'd draw hearts around his name in my spare time, and it was truly intoxicating. However, I was *not* making his heart race. I was clearly great at reading the signs because I managed to pluck up the courage to ask him to the school dance, because who says you need to wait for him to ask? *He said yes, we danced the night away, I had my first kiss and we lived happily ever after* ... Well, that's how it was meant to go. The reality was that he turned down my irresistible offer and asked my soon-to-be international model best friend instead, God knows why! But seriously, I wasn't sure what hurt more, that he asked my friend after turning me down or that she said yes knowing I wanted to go with him. I think it was the latter, because although I thought I was in love with him, it was her I loved more, and she was the one who was truly able to break my heart. Despite being obsessed with boys, I still had the Girl Power feelings in me and so the shock of being let down by one of my own friends stuck with me more than some boy turning me down. At nine years old, the excitement of getting attention from the opposite sex is too blinding to prioritise friendship, but there was something in my mind that knew the situation felt off and I wished it had played out differently. If it had been up to me at the time, she would have said no, choosing our friendship over a boy. I ended up going to the dance with another boy 'as friends', but maybe Keisha and I could have gone together and boycotted the whole idea! The thing is, now looking back, who's to say she didn't secretly really like him too and who was I to take away her happiness just because I had been rejected? Little did I know that this would be my first of many difficult experiences to come out of balancing friendships with relationships, girlfriends with partners and two very different types of love.

I remember when we started talking about secondary schools I felt uncomfortable finding out that we'd be rated on our academic success and that this would split us up. We started looking at different schools based on where we would realistically get into and because of where we lived and our academic abilities, we all ended up in different places. Our last day of school was

<u>Secrets</u>

I fancy a boy in 6C called Aaron. He's really fit. I asked him to the dance, but he said no. Then my friend asked him and he said yes. I'm really angry with her. It's keisha, one of my best friends.

emotional to say the least; all the classes in the year spent the day signing each other's school T-shirts, crying and hugging. The four of us sat on a bench in the playground and in true 'us' style decided to start singing. We sang the songs from our Year Six production of *Oliver!* and before we knew it we were joined by almost everyone in the year. Watching the VHS back of this final day, us sitting on the bench singing and laughing with everyone joining in, reminds me why I always tell people that I would go back to primary school in a heartbeat and that it was where I made some of my best memories and of course, the best of friends.

As we moved into our teens and moved on to different schools the friendship group dynamic changed yet again. It was never a question as to whether we'd stay in touch, but all of a sudden, we could only see each other on weekends or occasionally after school. SJ made a really close friend at her new school and I remember feeling insanely jealous; everyone referred to them as 'best friends' and it broke my heart. Despite my jealous feelings, we'd always make the effort to introduce each other to new friends and we made sure not to be exclusive. But our time spent together on weekends became less about making up dance routines to B*Witched and more about who could have the best 'evening in' on a Saturday night and invite the most boys. The teenage hormones felt impossible to control, I was so aware of my irrational emotions but felt helpless in controlling how I felt. If you read my diaries from the age of 13 to 15, the feelings and thoughts I shared are actually quite similar to those you often feel as an adult, but feeling them for the first time and not understanding them, mixed with crazy teenage hormones, makes for a very dramatic and emotional time. Jealousy can become a huge problem within friendships: jealousy of a new friend or love interest, jealousy of material items or of success. Jealousy can be an all-consuming emotion and it can even prevent you entering into a new friendship in the first place. I spoke to someone recently who's in their early twenties who told me they don't like to make new female friends as it just brings out their biggest insecurities and they always find themselves feeling jealous and unhappy around them. To me that is such a sad thought, that our own insecurities can prevent us forming new friendships. As a teenager, jealousy would often creep in and I would feel panicked if my friends made new friends, like they were going to leave me behind, and I'd be angry, focusing on whether I was better or worse than this new friend. Jealousy can blind you to the truth; it's like having a little devil on your shoulder feeding you lies. If a boy chose a friend over me, I wouldn't think about her and how she felt, I'd focus on my loss and what I had done to deserve the rejection. I think jealousy is something that can often come from within *you* and not necessarily from the friendship, which is why it can take time to solve. It's more about self-improvement and learning how to feel happy for someone else rather than putting the blame on the person you're jealous of. In your teens, jealousy in friendships becomes the norm and how you come out the other side determines how you feel about your friendships going forward.

As we navigated our way through secondary school, the four of us always kept in touch, but there were times when some relationships within the group became stronger than others. The thing is when you're in a group there are always going to be moments of jealousy because equal closeness between friends is an unrealistic fantasy. There was one time that Keisha, SJ and I went on holiday with my parents and one evening, when SJ had gone to bed early, Keisha and I stayed up to play a card game called 'Spit'. We had a funny and silly moment and the next day we couldn't stop laughing about it and reliving our 'private joke'. SJ cried herself to sleep that night wanting to go home because she felt so left out. We'd all felt this way at some point throughout our friendship; I also remember struggling when Keisha and SJ (who we also called Ush) would spend time together without me, it was like the worst thing in the world had happened. But we never confronted each other about our feelings, we bottled them up or, in my case, wrote them in a diary. Now as an adult I know how

> Hey,
>
> Saturday night Tash had a party, right... it waz good but... SJ pulled Aaron!!! Yes that is the Aaron I have fancied since yr 5, for 4 years!!! I wasn't really angry at her cuz it was her 1st pull but I would ov if it wasn't. I love her though, friends are so much more important than boys, i just only hope SJ will realize that one day or she'd end up loosing a lot of friends. I really LOVE Aaron. It's been 4 years now, I think i'm aloud to say LOVE not fancy!!!
>
> wat shall I do...? I was crying at the party, like mad!!! Grrrr !!! ☹
>
> Luv
>
> Miss No Lover
>
> xxx

NB: to 'pull' meant to kiss

to deal with jealous feelings better, either by jokingly addressing it, which most the time when said out loud diminishes it before it turns into anything real, or by finding the root of that jealousy and owning it as my own problem to fix.

HOW TO BE A GOOD FRIEND 101

I don't believe that being a good friend is just part of your personality or something that just comes naturally to some but not to others, I think you can proactively make yourself a good friend. Sure, you can have certain qualities that lend themselves well, such as kindness, thoughtfulness and wisdom. But I think everyone has the potential to be a great friend if they want to. It's just as much about adjusting your own personality traits as it is about understanding other people's. I have found that observing the relationships around you can be really helpful when assessing your own. Watching my mum and how she behaved with her friends had a massive impact on the way I treated mine and still do today. I suppose, in a lot of ways, observing her relationships with her female friends showed me the real potential for friendships with

Dear Diary, If you look
back through this diary
you'll see loads of stuff
about me going out to c
ush + keish, but for the
past week keish + ush
have been seeing each other
without me. They are my
best friends eva, but i
don't want to carry on
being the one who's always
rejected! Somepeople may
say i'm jealous, but so
what if I am!!!

Help

lil xxxx

other women and just how important they are. My mum
has always been the friend who is patient and generous
with her time. Although my dad would describe it as
racking up the phone bill and gossiping, I would say she
performs a valuable role as the agony aunt of her

friendship group. She's always there to listen with absolute patience and give genuine advice when it's needed.

Before having kids, she had friends from her teenage days, who in more recent years she's reconnected with, but as she started to have kids her friendship group changed and most of her best friends now are the mums of my friends, or my sister's friends. I'm the youngest in my family and there is quite a big age gap between me and my eldest sister, so the friends my mum has through me are naturally a few years younger than her. As the eldest in her group of friends she's always taken on the role of the 'big sister friend' and through the celebrations and the harder times she's always been there for her girls. I can see from observing her friendship group that change is inevitable and throughout children, schooling, hormonal changes and divorces, they have always leant on each other for support.

Now, at 30, I am also able to give my mum advice on her friends and although we share the same values we often bring different perspectives to a situation, which can be helpful. I wouldn't describe my mum as my best friend – she's my mum – but we are incredibly close. We have the sort of closeness that isn't so much about hugging or saying, 'I love you', we're not a very touchy-feely family, but when I need her she'll drop anything to come. We speak every day, we choose to hang out on Saturday nights and she has the answer to any question no matter what time of day. *It's also worth mentioning that her chicken-soup-making skills are out of this world.* When it comes to friends, she has all the experience, so for the more complicated issues she always seems to know what's worth addressing and what's worth sweeping under the rug. I think because of my job and how exposed I am to different opinions and points of view online, I tend to bring her an alternative opinion when she speaks about her friends. I'll always try to see it from their perspective and give some advice on how to handle a situation fairly. I'm definitely more emotional, or as she would say 'deep', and things can upset me more than her; she's learnt over the years not to let others bring her down, so she can detach a friend's problem from her own. Seeing her be such a good friend to others has definitely made me more aware of what kind of friend I am.

One of my mum's longest-standing friendships is with her teenage best friend, Amanda. They grew up in the sixties so they'd spend their free time together shopping at Biba, clubbing, having sleepovers and helping each other iron their hair, *literally with the iron and an ironing board.* Amanda was always very creative and beautiful, and she had a really bubbly personality that would light up a room. They stayed close through their twenties and as they both went on to have kids, we'd always get together as families for birthdays and special occasions. It was during their fifties that my mum felt they were drifting apart as friends; she'd noticed a real lack of communication from Amanda and they didn't speak as often as they once did. She'd try to phone her but she'd never answer or she'd say she wasn't well and couldn't talk. For about a year, she'd tried to reach out but could never really pin Amanda down; she couldn't understand what had happened and whether she'd done something wrong, but she persevered. Eventually, after years of uncomfortable distance, Amanda invited her over and when she visited, she quite quickly discovered her friend had completely changed in all respects; she'd had a breakdown and had clearly been struggling. I think at first my mum didn't know how to react and felt like she'd lost a part of her friend, but she never ran away from it, she stayed and gave as much support as she could.

Her illness led to Amanda losing most of her 'every-day' friends, because through no fault of her own, she'd lost the ability to care for others as much and every-thing became very much about her. My mum stood by her though, always having the utmost patience in listen-ing to her express how she felt no matter how irrational her thoughts might have been, and she gradually became her confidante, taking on a new role as a friend. She'd be there for the good days but also for the bad, helping to support her and those around her. It was never easy for my mum; just going into the hospitals was quite a traumatic experience. I have always admired her patience, her strength and the kindness she has shown to those going through harder times. I think it's easy for people to run away from a scary situation, not knowing how to deal with it or not wanting to, but she never did that. Seeing her relationship with Amanda adapt over the years has taught me to have patience, to be caring and to try to be a more selfless friend.

She has individual friends who require more one-on-one attention from her but she also has a tight group of girlfriends. She's made lots of different friends through-out my life and seeing how she brings them together is something I've always wanted to embrace myself. Even now, in their sixties, her group of girlfriends take an annual trip together and it's something I really hope my friends and I adopt too. One thing I've noticed when observing their friendship group is that jealousy is no longer an issue at all. I think as you create your own life and family you become content with what you've got and a friend's gain no longer feels like your loss.

It was in my twenties that I started to learn how to be happy for my friends, and not only did it strengthen my friendships but selfishly, it made me a much happier person too. Feeling jealous, angry and frustrated is exhausting and realising that I had the power to control how I felt about my friends changed everything. It wasn't anything particular that changed my way of thinking, possibly just a coming of age, and I think I just started to express my happiness for others and literally say it out loud, which is when I noticed what a positive impact it had on my attitude. I started to be really aware of the kind of friend I was to others, which is something I think is important to reflect on. Up until that point I had very much focused on how my friends treated me. Did they message me enough? Did they ever leave me out? Did they invite me to their party? Were they always honest with me? The focus was on *their* role as a friend. When you're younger it's all a bit petty and the arguments are quite insignificant but as I grew up I found the negative parts of my friendships felt more intense and I became more aware of how I treated my friends, what kind of friend they saw in me and what little changes I could make to bring us even closer together. Strengthening those friendships and committing to them as a long-term relationship was something I became really passionate about.

THE RECIPE FOR A GOOD FRIENDSHIP

Ingredients
125g loyalty
140g empathy, melted
2 cups of support
110g trust
2 litres self-confidence
150g time

Method
1. Keep the oven at a cool 100°C with no sudden temperature changes.
2. Line the tray with self-confidence before laying loyalty down on top, making sure no arguments ever stick.
3. Beat together the empathy and support until thick and pour onto tray making sure it's even.
4. Sift over the trust.
5. Let it cook evenly and always allow for cooling down.

One of the most obvious ways that you can become a better friend is by learning from experiences that have affected you personally. When a friend treats you badly it can be heartbreaking but the positive thing you can take from it is knowing how it feels and making sure you never put one of your friends in the same position. It's quite a mature way of thinking but what you dish out comes back to you tenfold. Learning from my friends' strengths and weaknesses, appreciating their gestures and acknowledging when something they've said or done has hurt me has helped me to become a more conscientious friend. Maybe you have a friend who constantly points out the negative in a situation, so it makes you more aware of keeping a realistic but positive balance in how you communicate with friends. On a more selfish note, it's also made *me* feel better in general. Jealousy, bitterness and paranoia are horrible feelings to have running through your mind, so finding peace and a way not to feel those is a real relief.

Treat your friends how you would like to be treated yourself is something I think about all the time. What I look for in a friend is someone I can rely on, who I know will be there for me at the drop of a hat if I really need them; someone who will listen and be honest with me if I ask for their advice, but also has empathy and knows how best to comfort me. I also like to feel as though I take some kind of priority for them and, finally, I want my friends to feel like they can open up to me and show their raw selves.

Knowing how to be there for a friend is something I've learnt over time. At seven years old one of my best friends had to deal with her parents splitting up and understandably, as I was her closest friend at the time and her desk partner at school, she took it out on me. I didn't understand how she was feeling, I didn't even really understand the situation, all I knew was that my best friend had poked me in the arm with a pencil before drawing a line down the middle of the desk and telling me never to cross it because she no longer wanted to be my friend. That night my mum had to sit me down to tell me that she didn't mean it and that she was going through a hard time at home. She told me how sometimes when we're upset we take it out on the people closest to us. It was my responsibility to be grown up about it, not to make it about myself but instead to be there for her and support her when she needed it most. I was only seven so I didn't exactly sit her down and give her advice but I remember just trying my hardest not to get upset by anything she was saying to me and I just kept quiet, waiting for her to feel better in her own time. I think at that age controlling your emotions is really hard but I had to remind myself it wasn't really about me. I realised over time that being a fun friend worked as a good distraction, so we never spoke about what happened but instead I was something positive she could focus on during school times.

At 14 years old, I witnessed true bullying for the first time when one of my closest friends was repeatedly being teased for the way she looked. We'd met outside of school through mutual friends and so the bullying wasn't something I was aware of at first. It started when she was 13; the boys would call her names in the playground or walk past her classroom making faces through the glass. At first it was just the boys and as she was friendly with the popular girls she just about managed to ignore it, but during the next year of school things just got worse. The girls began to care more about what the boys thought and desperately wanted to impress them, so they'd distance themselves from her, some even joining in on the bullying.

She felt so isolated and alone that she started to find any excuse to take time off school. She told me that one time she faked breaking her wrist, using information she'd found online to pretend she'd broken the one tiny bone that can't be seen on X-rays. When she was at school she'd cry in the toilets, phoning her mum begging her to pick her up, and if her mum was at work, she'd phone a friend's mum, who'd pick her up and have her at her house in the meantime. It was excuse after excuse and eventually her mum gave up trying to convince her to go in, but missing so much school meant she gradually lost any friendships she once had and she was dropped from the netball team, the one thing she actually enjoyed doing at school. She decided to leave that school and moved to another where it happened all over again.

When I looked at her I saw a girl with the most incredible hair that I was insanely jealous of, perfectly groomed French manicure nails and the most contagious smile; she was my fun teenage friend who had me in stitches laughing. So, when we were on summer camp together and I saw the bullying with my own eyes and heard the name-calling right there in front of me, it truly shocked and confused me. At that age, you're not used to being selfless, you're wrapped up in your own little world of who you fancy at school or what your parents did to annoy you; it's difficult to step up and be the hero in an unfamiliar situation. Honestly, if this happened today, I would have reacted completely differently, I would have stuck up for her right then and there and put that teenage boy in his place. I would have spoken to an adult in charge and told them what was going on, but at the time I simply chose to support her as a friend and I think that was enough. I knew what was right and wrong but I wasn't confident enough to act upon something by myself. Now I've grown into someone who would always stand up for someone else, but at that time I didn't want the bullies to win so I just tried to shower her with as much love and support as I could at the time, trying to counteract what was going on elsewhere. Confrontation isn't always the answer and I like to think that being there for her, although it didn't stop the bullying, made the situation a little easier.

When I spoke to her recently she said that our friendship, as well as others she had out of school, was her lifeline during that time. She lived for the weekend, making Saturday night plans on a Monday morning, and just wanted to spend as much time as she could around the people who were nice and made her feel good about herself. So maybe the hero isn't always the one to stick up for you and who confronts the bullies, maybe just being a good friend can sometimes be enough, it's just a different kind of hero.

'Firsts' are a major part of growing up, especially in your teens – the first time you witness bullying is up there as one of the worst kinds of firsts, but then there are the happy memories that come from your first experiences. And there is something to be said about the friends you make during those times. My friend Gemma and I met at a family friend's party when we were 12; we snuck away from the marquee in the garden, sat in the living room and giggled whilst we sipped on a smuggled glass of champagne. It set the scene for our friendship really as we went on to experience all the firsts together. Maybe it's because she was a new friend that it felt different; although I felt 100% comfortable with my childhood friends, the excitement of making a new friend as a teenager meant we were more rebellious together as we tried to navigate through our teens. I tried my first cigarette with her, we lost our virginity around the same time, went on holiday without our parents, made many makeup mistakes together and unfortunately discovered the joys of a hangover. It was because of all of these experiences that we became such incredibly close friends; being able to show your vulnerability when doing something for the very first time bonds you together and builds a huge amount of trust within a friendship. It meant that no matter what hurdles life might throw at us, we always have this tight connection.

One of my favourite memories with Gemma was New Year's Eve just as we were heading into 2015; it was just before midnight and I have no idea why but we found ourselves in the toilet of the flat we were having a party in. New Year's Eve always gives me that excited buzz for the year ahead but that year we knew something big was coming her way; we looked each other in the eye, held hands and jumped up and down screaming with excitement. It came out of nowhere and when we walked out the toilet to confused-looking faces we just looked at each other, laughed and said 'it was nothing'. That year she got engaged and we both knew it was coming. I always think back to that night because all those years later and we're still celebrating our 'firsts' together.

... the one who's always there to give you advice

THE OLDER SISTER FRIEND

She's the friend to speak to when you have a dilemma. She'll listen to your worries and won't reply with her own problems. She *actually* listens and gives you solid advice. She probably doesn't open up to you as much, she'll have her own older sister friend to speak to, but you're close enough that she doesn't get offended if you spend half an hour talking about yourself and she enjoys being your shoulder to cry on. She seems to have experienced it all before and she'll teach you how to learn from her mistakes. If someone breaks your heart she'll be the first one to march over there and tell him he's been an asshole. She'll plan your hen party and announce that she knows you the best *by far*! The older sister friend is the one you can be totally honest with, even when it comes to talking about awkward topics like your salary. There's zero competition, she'll always be there to help you grow and she has the ability to enjoy your success without thinking of it as a failure for herself. The older sister friend is pretty much family – you might as well get matching tattoos.

Do: *Open up and be raw with her. You can trust her to be on your side.*

Don't: *Forget to give back to the friendship, asking her how she is so it isn't always about you and your problems.*

GENERATIONAL
FRIENDSHIP

I come from a big family of women. My grandma was one of five daughters, she then had two daughters, her kids had six daughters between them, three of whom were my sisters and me, so until my sisters started popping out all the boys we were a female-dominated family. As it stands the youngest girl in the family is my niece Honey, who's five, and the eldest is my grandma Teresa, who is 87; for obvious reasons, both have very different things to say about female friendships. Honey, who's in Year One of primary school, is only just getting started when it comes to making friends, although it blows my mind to think I was only her age when I met some of my best friends. And then there's my grandma, who has a lifetime of experience; some of her friends are sadly no longer alive but some she still sees regularly, meeting up for coffees or going for walks together. I sat down to chat to both my niece and my grandma about their female friendships and to ask them similar questions as a bit of an experiment to see how our opinions change over time and what we learn.

I FaceTimed Honey before her bedtime and, after giving it a bit of thought, she gave me the go-ahead to ask her some questions. It turned out she'd only answer my questions by whispering the answers into my sister's ear, who then told me what she'd said, so here are the results from our Chinese Whispers – oh, the joys of interviewing a five-year-old . . .

Honey, I want to know, do you have one *best* friend or do you have lots of good friends?

I have one best friend, Kíla.

And when did you meet her?

In Reception, we were in the same class.

What do you like about your best friend?

She makes me happy and she's my best, best friend. She's nice, she's not bossy and she has nice skin. We pick games to play together.

Do you think you're a good friend to her and why?

Yes, because I'm kind, I'm helpful, I share and I bought her a friendship bracelet from holiday.

Has a friend ever made you sad or have you ever had a fight?

No. Never. (We suspect she just doesn't want to tell us!)

And what's the nicest thing your friend has ever done for you?

She bought me a birthday present. And when we play 'mummies and daddies', she always lets me be the mummy.

I popped over to my grandma's flat for tea because, although she might look twenty years younger than she is, she hasn't got the best hearing so I thought we'd have a face-to-face chat (and also because she gives the best hugs). I often speak to her about her family that I didn't get to meet or about my mum's upbringing before I came along, but I've never really spoken to her about her friends and I realised instantly that she is *just* like my mum, she's also the 'older sister friend'.

OK, first question, do you believe in having one *best* friend or lots of good friends?

I think it's good to have a few different friends; I had four best friends. Two were French, one lived locally, still does, and the other I met at work. One was German, who I met because she married your grandpa's friend, and the other is English but we met because our daughters were friends in school.

If you had to pick one *best* friend, could you?

No not really, they were all different and I'd go to them for different things. My sister Jessie was probably my best friend, she was five years older than me and I adored her but sadly she died in a car crash when she was only 37. We always had a strong bond and connection, she was fun and spontaneous; she always had trouble with men and once she came to live with me after a break-up, which I just loved. It was different with her than with my friends because the love was unconditional, I was her baby sister.

What qualities do you think a best friend needs to have?

My friends were all slightly different but then they all had one thing in common: they were interesting. I always gravitate towards slightly quirky women, I had lots of friends in fashion and showbiz. I think it's important as friends to enjoy the same way of life, to be able to socialise well with each other, and I think it's important for you to be able to be honest with each other. Although I have learnt over the years that a little white lie can sometimes be important to protect a friendship, you know, to keep them happy. You learn to accept their flaws, so if someone is a jealous character and you know that from the start then you just make it work and know how to act with them – they can't help who they are!

Do you think you're a good friend and why?

Yes, I think I am because I'm patient and I'm honest.

I remember when we used to go out as a group for dinner, the other girls would always make me walk into the restaurant first, it was so silly. They'd always come to me for life advice or even just for fashion advice! One of my oldest friends gets very stressed about certain situations and I'm the only one who can speak to her honestly and she'll listen to me.

What's the worst experience you've had with a female friend?

I once had a friend who was very jealous, which was difficult. She worked in a beautiful high-end fashion boutique and I was out of work; she knew a colleague was leaving so she got me a job and I was thrilled. But when I started working there and was doing well at my job, getting praise from the manager, she became jealous and would bitch about me behind my back to the other managers or say nasty things to me. I was so confused, but actually once we got to know each other better I realised how her mind worked so I knew how to behave with her and she knew me better so didn't feel jealous or threatened anymore.

What's the best memory you have with a friend?

Oh, there were so many. We'd always have parties on New Year's Eve, my girlfriends and all of our husbands would get together and we'd take turns cooking, there would be music and games. One of my favourite memories was with my sister Jessie, we went on holiday to Italy, just me, her and your mother, and we had the best time.

There's something so beautifully naïve about Honey liking her best friend because of her skin but then there's also something so true about my grandma accepting that no one is perfect and that if it takes a few white lies to maintain your friendships then that's OK. It was bittersweet talking about her sister Jessie and we both had a little cry, but it did make me think more about friendships between sisters because for some, they trump any other kind of female friendship. She loved all of her sisters but the age gap was so big with some they felt more like mother figures and then with others they just had very different lives and social circles to her. But she and Jessie just clicked; maybe it was their five-year age gap or that their personalities just matched up well, but for her the friendship they had was stronger than any other. But whilst most people probably do love their sisters, it's not always the case that sisterly relationships extend beyond mere family ties.

SISTER, SISTER!

'There's a point in every friendship where friends stop being friends and become sisters': a quote I see floating around Instagram often. And it's true, best friends over time do become more like sisters, but then does this just apply to those who don't already have sisters? And if best friends do become 'sisters', do they replace the real sisters? There are some who see them as two completely separate roles and others who believe a sister truly can also be a best friend.

I'm the youngest of three girls, so when it comes to sisters I have all the experience, *but* having spoken to others I've quickly realised it is completely different for us all. When my pending existence was announced the news was welcomed with less-than-open arms; my sisters, who were seven and ten, packed a suitcase full of crisps and cuddly toys and planned their runaway escape. They didn't get very far as getting down the stairs without being caught proved more difficult than they'd thought, but it's fair to say they weren't too pleased about my arrival. As they always say, you can't choose your family. They were happy once they met me and were *thrilled* to be able to pick my middle name (hence the *Flintstones* reference) but because I was so much younger than both of them, it took a long time for me to even be in the position for us to be friends. For so long I was just the annoying younger sister who would beg to join in when they had friends over, only to be turned away and told I was too young. We always had fun on holidays together and we were definitely close, but I wouldn't say it ever felt like a friendship until I was about 15, when I started to get invited to their birthday parties and I felt I could interact more with their friends without embarrassing them. I started to develop my own confidence and personality traits and I'd be more aware of theirs.

Now that we're all grown up, the dynamic is definitely interesting, to say the least. Carly, the eldest, and Jojo, the middle one, have quite a fiery relationship because they are closer in age, completely different in personalities and I personally think they care for each other in a different way and have a different type of bond because of the long period of time during which it was just the two of them. Carly is very organised, a slight control freak (we have that in common) who can be very rational with her decisions and Jojo is a complete Gemini who wears her heart on her sleeve, isn't afraid to be spontaneous and has the tendency to be quite irrational with her thoughts. Then there's me, the youngest but a complete mix of the two, who often sits right in the middle when it comes to family arguments.

I think because of the age difference Carly has always been more motherly and protective of me, whereas Jojo and I have been able to have slightly more of a friendship, but I tend to spend equal time with them just having very different kinds of conversations with the two. My relationship with Carly is more typical of a sister; she will often give me advice and use examples of things she's experienced to help me make decisions, she'll ask me how the book-writing is going and suggest introducing me to a friend who's written a book before. Whereas my relationship with Jojo is more casual; we'll talk about things we've seen on social media or laugh about something silly the kids did. I'll often give her advice when she's not seeing the bigger picture and it's nice for me that I'm now able to have the 'advice-giving' role too. But there's no denying that both my sisters have certain traits that I wouldn't usually look for in a friend, and I'm sure they'd have something to say about my bad traits too. But the difference between sisters and friends is that I've learnt to accept their flaws because being close with my sisters is important to me, especially when it comes to kids and the next generation in our family. Although Jojo and Carly can be so different at times, their children are best friends and so they'll always put their differences aside to let those new family friendships blossom.

We often hear about sisters who are best friends though, whether that's in a teenage novel or on our favourite TV show, but I don't think that's always the case; I would say my sisters are my sisters, not my best friends. We have a friendship that's unique, but it certainly differs from the ones I have with my friends because at the end of the day we are stuck together. Our arguments are fleeting because we all know that by tomorrow we will have forgotten all about it and moved on. Over the years my sisters have got to know my female friends and it's made us closer that we can socialise together and they can be more involved in my life outside of family events. They've known some of my friends for so long that they're almost like family, and the relationship my sisters have with my friends is really comforting to me.

But there definitely are some sisters who are best friends, who don't need anyone but each other and wouldn't have it any other way. I knew two girls growing up who were only a year apart in age and were always inseparable. They'd wear matching clothes as kids, share friends as teenagers and in their twenties, chose to move into a flat together. And if this is your reality than I say, why not? Having your sister as your best friend can be great for so many reasons . . .

- She already knows all of your most embarrassing stories and your worst habits
- She'll take the piss out of you but won't let anyone else do the same
- Your age gap means you experience different things at different times in your life, so you can help each other with advice
- You can be totally honest with each other without taking offence
- She'll get the giggles with you at boring family events

- You can be real with your emotions and have raging arguments if you want, without the risk of losing each other
- She finishes your sentences for you
- The boundaries are flexible; you can be as close or as distant as you like (physically and emotionally) without it being weird or needing an explanation
- You take each other's approval seriously, meaning all new friends and boyfriends must be approved first
- You're totally protective of each other; you always have her back and she always has yours

I spoke to two other friends who are also the youngest of three girls and because of the difference in age gaps, we all have slightly different relationships with our sisters, although the roles all seem to be the same. The eldest is always the most together and organised, the middle is usually the wild one (but probably the most fun) and the youngest is the peacekeeper. My friend Jada has a close relationship with both of her sisters but whilst her eldest is more like a big sister, the middle sister is her *best* friend. They speak every day, she'll call her whilst walking home from work and they tell each other everything. There are only three years between them, which seems like the perfect age gap to me as it's not too big that they're in completely different life stages but then it's not *so* close that it's competitive. The way she speaks about her sister, like no friend would ever compete, is so nice. Knowing your best friend is so secure, that she's definitely not going anywhere – she's literally family – must be so comforting. I think the relationships she has with her sisters are really special and I know she doesn't take them for granted.

My friend Rosie has five years between her and her middle sister and they also get on the best out of the three. Whilst the eldest sister was at university, the middle sister took her under her wing and was there for her when she had her first kiss, tried her first cigarette and had her first break-up. Now that they're older she can bond with both, speaking to the eldest sister about the more 'adulting' topics like her career and living situation. But because of the time she spent growing up with the middle sister, their bond has always been closer. When I asked how she felt the friendships she has with her sisters differ from those with her friends she said that her sisters just know her like the backs of their hands. Sisters know when you're unhappy before you even know and they'll be more aware of your emotions because they've grown up with you. Sometimes my sisters just look at me and say, 'What's wrong?' and it'll make me cry about something I didn't even know I was upset about. She said their feedback and advice, although cutting at times, is always honest and real because there's no risk of falling out and never recovering from it. They always want the best for her with no ulterior motive, so she knows she can trust them 100%. One time whilst her sister was pregnant she planned to have her over for dinner and had spent the whole day preparing, ready to spoil her, when her sister phoned to cancel. She was so upset but instead of holding back and saying, 'No worries,' like maybe she would have done with friends, she said, 'I've spent the whole day preparing and I really wanted to do this for you, I'm so annoyed.' Her sister replied, 'I'm pregnant and I want to go to bed, we'll do it another time,' as blunt and upfront as sisters can be. She thought, *Fair enough*, and that was that. Something that might have brewed for months into a larger argument was addressed then and there and dealt with, and that's really what sisters are all about.

Whether you are best friends, just close friends or occasionally get to see each other at family events, the friendship we have with our sisters is special and there's no denying they have their earned place amongst our female friendships.

#AskLP

I'm 24 and don't have any long-term friends. I make new friendships and most of the time they'll last 2/3 years max. I wonder if my personality is the problem or if it is because I don't go out as much as other people because of my anxiety. People usually like me, they say I'm funny and all, but they don't get attached to the point of wanting me in their life forever.

I think it's normal to have friendships that last 2/3 years, because we are constantly changing and growing all the time so it's not always the case that those friends grow at the same pace. I think the fact that you make new friends easily is great, that's half the battle! When I feel like a friend is becoming distant I try to make an effort to stay in touch by messaging or calling them, asking if they want to catch up. It doesn't matter how long it's been; if there was a connection once before, it can be there again. I wouldn't blame your anxiety, but maybe if it's something you're self-conscious of you should try to open up to your friends about it. They might have similar feelings, or if you tell them how you feel then at least they'll know what you're thinking instead of assuming they know. Maybe they think you don't like hanging out with them when really, it's just because you feel anxious in certain situations; I'm sure they'll be understanding. I always think that opening up to a friend, although it feels like a risk, can often bring you closer together and make you more attached.

FINDING LOVE FROM A 'FRIEND FLIRT'

Making a new friend is like falling in love. It's the best feeling when you find yourself ignoring everyone else in the room and only talking to her because she's just so fascinating. I've never really been the sort of person whose real first impressions are based on what someone looks like. All of my previous boyfriends were made after getting to know them and being friends beforehand, as it's always been personalities rather than looks that have really stood out to me. Now, when I'm in the situation where I'm with a lot of women, the ones who usually grab my attention will have a group of people around them laughing or are lighting up the room in some way. Maybe they've spilt their drink and followed it up with a self-deprecating comment or they're the first one to put their hand up at a Q&A event. I've always been surrounded by confident, gutsy women so it's a trait I always seem to look for in a friend.

When you meet someone great who draws you in, you may think you have found someone special and possibly someone who's going to be significant in your life, but asking for her number or adding her on Facebook is as nerve-wracking as a first date. Making plans to meet up can be genuinely terrifying; you get that buzz knowing you have so much to talk about because you're essentially starting from scratch but you wonder if the chemistry will burn out, if you'll run out of things to say and if she'll start to actually find you quite annoying. You want to take her to all of your favourite places, but is tomorrow too soon to text her when you've spent the whole day hanging out? Friendship dating is daunting but it's also fun, it's exciting and there's no doubt that it can turn into true friend-love.

THE DOS AND DON'TS ON A FRIEND DATE

Do be the first to initiate a date. She won't think you're too forward, she'll admire your confidence to make the first move.

OMG she wants to meet up, **don't** freak out.

Do suggest a very cool pop-up outdoor food market with cocktails.

Don't tell her your whole life story within the first 20 minutes.

Do follow up the date with interesting links and cute memes on topics you discussed on said date.

Don't tell her you love her on the first date no matter how tempting 'Uh, I just love you' is.

Do show an interest in something you've seen that she's been up to but **don't** expose too much about your Instagram stalking. **Don't** refer to anything you've seen on her Instagram stories in the past 24 hours.

Do compliment her on what she's wearing but be specific; 'I love your outfit' just won't cut it!

Don't spend the whole time talking about how great your other friends are.

Do follow up post-date, maybe suggest a class or workshop to sign up to so you can get to know each other better.

Don't, I repeat **don't**, ask for a selfie on the first date.

My friend Grace was forced into a friend date as a teenager, almost like a grown-up play date, and the experience left her terrified of future friend dates. She was 14 and she'd just moved from London to a small village where she didn't know anyone. Her mum had joined a gardening club, made friends with another mum and they became obsessed with the idea of introducing their daughters to each other. Neither daughter felt particularly keen, but a dinner was set up nonetheless, with the parents in one room eating and the 'kids' in another, to get to know each other. She said it was the most awkward evening she'd ever experienced, because no matter how they tried, they had nothing in common, they didn't gel together and apart from their mums being friends there was zero common ground. They sat in silence watching *X Factor*, desperately waiting for the evening to end and when it did, they never spoke again.

As teenagers, I think we find it particularly difficult to make small talk, which really is key to getting a friend date going at first. My friend Debs used to work in sales and she'd regularly speak on the phone to the different businesses she looked after. There was one restaurant that she'd phone almost every day, desperately trying to get hold of the owner but having to speak to the manager instead. The manager was American and always very friendly on the phone, and Debs was encouraged to be extra friendly on calls, so she was, and this led to them talking quite a bit, which they both really enjoyed. They'd talk casually about boyfriends, work, food and then Haley, the manager, mentioned how she didn't really know anyone in London yet since moving. After speaking for a few weeks Haley asked if she'd like to meet for a coffee and Debs thought there wasn't much to lose, so she did! She was quite excited at the idea of meeting someone completely new and unlinked to anyone she knew and she already felt like she knew her quite well from speaking on the phone. The date was fun, they chatted away with no awkward silences, Haley was extremely confident, which threw Debs a bit, but it went well and they even arranged to meet up again for brunch. A few weeks later they had brunch, an equally successful friend date, and they talked about doing it again sometime. But life got in the way and with the busyness of their individual lives and the attention their existing friends required, neither pursued the friendship, so it wasn't able to turn into something real. Maybe the learning is that just like romantic dating, you might have to kiss a few frogs before you find your prince. Getting the right chemistry with someone is important and just because you get on, doesn't mean you're going to become great friends. Debs looks back on the experience with nice memories and although it didn't work out, she was glad she took the chance on some-one new.

Just like with any other date, if there's a connection, you'll know it. Falling in love with a new friend is the best, not only because the right friend can help shape the person you become, but also because the right friend can affect the quality of your romantic relationships. My husband and I are not the most confrontational people, we're good at discussing issues but more often than not we'll leave it before it esca-lates into something bigger. But I have found myself on multiple occasions confiding in my friend Hannah for advice when something in my relationship might be playing on my mind; usually it'll be something more specific to *my* actions or feelings. I find it really helps to have a more neutral perspective on things and she'll help me see a situation from a different angle. We take long walks and talk honestly about our feelings, which means that I can avoid saying things I don't mean and if something is worth confronting, I can do so in a more thoughtful, calm way. The love I have for my friends has always been important and intertwined with my relationship with Rich.

When I first got engaged I wasn't really sure what the first steps of wedding planning involved. I had all the usual questions: how many people will you invite? Which venue will you choose? Will you take his name? I didn't know any of that yet. But the first thing I did, which at the time I didn't really think much of, was send out handwritten cards to my sisters and closest girlfriends to tell them what they mean to me and to make it clear that I wanted them to somehow be a part of the process and the day. It sounds a bit weird but at a time when I felt so happy and in love, I wanted to share that with all the other people whose love was also important to me.

Romance and love is rarely associated with friendship, but the love between friends can also be passionate and emotional; this also became evident to me on my hen weekend during a dinner that I'll never forget. My very excitable friend thought it would be a nice idea to go around the table and ask my friends one by one to tell the story of how we met and express what I mean to them. They went first and then it was my turn to say what they all individually mean to me. Let me just set the scene for you . . . ten grown women, most of whom were in their late twenties, uncontrollably crying (some were definitely sobbing), as we literally poured our love onto each other. It was spontaneous, raw and most importantly, it was a great example of how important female friendship is to us all. Just like romantic love, the love shared between friends can be hard to describe, but sitting and actually expressing our feelings to one another like this was one of the most romantic things that's ever happened to me.

SISTERHOOD

You choose the arms of who you fall into
It's no mistake or divine fate
I untangled mine that had been long folded
Extended to wipe tears from your face
But you bolted the door and made other calls
And decided he could be both lover and mate
It is pain bursting, heart hurting, panic searing
I'd long boxed and put away
But you pressured my elbows back to my sides
And now I comfort and cradle my own waist
I loved you much deeper than boys ever knew
Put moments of future and happiness with you
Into multi-coloured knots that we wore on our
    wrists
But you pulled off our chains when you chose to
    grab his

I didn't know kinship in ways that we found
Could speak in a language that held such foreign
   sound
Of missed calls and unread texts
I just pray you recognise my heartbreak
When one day he becomes your ex
– Charly Cox

. . . AND THEN SHE
BROKE MY HEART

A friend of mine once told me this story of hers, 'Want to know why I struggle to trust women?' she said.

Everything was going wrong for her, one thing after the other, as if her life was falling apart in front of her very eyes. The end of a difficult relationship had resulted in a living situation she couldn't afford; this added immense pressure to her job and without any family living nearby she was incredibly lonely. She felt more alone than ever, sitting on the sofa eating baked potatoes for dinner every night. She started doubting her future and wondering if moving away from her family to be in London had been really worth it. You know when you want so badly for there to be a shift and for something good to come your way? Well, after months of feeling like it never would, relief finally came in the form of an old school friend. It seemed as though this familiar face had come along at just the right time; she gave her the motivation and self-worth she so badly needed at a time when she was feeling completely helpless. The old school friend offered a solution: they should move in together! It was the perfect plan, they'd move in and become even closer friends and would focus their twenties on enjoying city life and climbing the career ladder, supporting each other on the way up. They spent an evening together celebrating, sipping champagne, tucking into overpriced macaroons and trawling the Internet looking for the perfect home to move into. The night was filled with anticipation, fun, laughter and excitement – it was the happiest she'd felt in a long time. But the next day when she tried to continue the excitement over text and set things in motion, she was met with nothing in return. It was as if the night before hadn't happened and she wondered how things could suddenly feel so different. She endured weeks of unanswered calls and one-sided text conversations until a text finally came through: 'I've decided to move in with someone else, hope you understand.' She didn't. How could she possibly understand? After ignoring her for weeks, she finally gets in touch and completely lets her down, shattering the only future plans that had lifted her spirits in months. How could she lift her so high and then drop her without any warning? *Did I do something wrong? How could I not have seen this coming? What am I going to do now? How do I respond? Where am I going to live? How could she care so little for my feelings?* They never spoke again.

So, she doesn't trust women and, well, it all makes sense to me now. The lack of trust and loyalty in that relationship left her feeling completely doubtful of all her past and future friendships. I asked her how it has affected her making friends since, to which she told me that she rarely makes them. Unless she's forced into a situation whereby she spends a lot of time with someone, like at work, where they can prove their loyalty to her over time, a female friendship is not something she actively looks for. She'll never make the effort to pursue a new friendship because she doesn't want to be let down again and feel the disappointment that she's felt in the past.

Heartbreak is often something associated with romantic relationships, but the love of a friend can be just as incredible as love with a romantic partner, and therefore the heartbreak is just as painful. At least with a break-up it can be emotional and confrontational; sometimes when friendships end it can be without much explanation at all. Maybe she just started to ignore your messages? Or started bitching about you behind your back? Without much warning, there can be a shift that suddenly turns things sour and for some reason it's not confronted. The commitment and label of 'partner' or 'husband and wife' means that an ending needs to be confirmed, these titles need action to be taken in order to remove them. But we're a lot more fickle with our friendships and the term 'friend' is loosely thrown around, so there often doesn't seem to be a definitive start or end. We put so much time and effort into our friendships but when things get tough they can be dropped and given up on so easily.

My friend's experience was a particularly traumatic one but I think we've all experienced being let down by a girlfriend before, whether it's feeling like you're constantly put second or being truly heartbroken by a friend's betrayal. Is it just me who's blacklisted certain female names from future baby- or pet-name lists because it reminds me of that girl who was awful to me? It can also be the little things that let you down; being disorganised or flaky is a trait many people have and I don't think they mean for it to affect others but if a friend is constantly late or cancelling plans last minute you can feel like you're not a priority to them. Not returning a phone call may not seem like a big deal to some, but being a good friend means putting yourself in their frame of mind and being considerate of their feelings. A friend who lets you down, no matter if it's in a big or small way, is a disappointing friend.

Putting your trust in the wrong person can leave you scarred and unable to open up and try again. There are so many ways that a friend can let you down: by not being there for you during a hard time, by using you to get somewhere only to drop you once they do, or by constantly cancelling plans and flaking out. I think a lot of women struggle to trust other women whether it's due to the way female relationships can be portrayed by the media or due to their own negative experiences.

For me, primary school was a breeze when I think about it, but the first time I really experienced 'cattiness' was at secondary school within the intensity of an all-girls school. It wouldn't have been my first choice, having grown up enjoying male friends, but I was lured in by the idea of no school uniform and at the time didn't think it being an all-girls school would be an issue. Secondary school was hard; it was the first time that I felt different and as if I didn't fit in. My former confident self turned shy and I felt insecure without my girls around me. When you're faced with people who have very different values to you, the natural connection doesn't happen and the friend-making process feels a lot more forced. My primary school was larger with a huge mix of ethnic backgrounds and somehow that made the playing field feel level, but at this new school it felt very much like 'me against the rest'.

Because of the no-uniform rule, the first day was less about who you got on with and more about what you looked like. I grew to love having no uniform and used it as a way to express myself and to be comfortable – it's not something I look back on with regret – but in those early years it definitely divided us by how we chose to dress and, for some, what they could afford to buy. I made friends but felt really aware of how different they were to the ones I'd made previously and I never felt like I could completely be myself. I'd become so used to spending time with the same people who totally understood me, but now if I made a really sarcastic comment I'd be misunderstood and alienated from a group. I became paranoid about my own personality traits and how much of my true self I could share.

There were moments of real friendship; I was one of the first in my class to start my period so when some of the other girls also started they came straight to me for advice. It was nice to feel closer to them and to feel like I could help them in some way and that they could trust me. There were some really strong friendships within our year but I couldn't identify with any of them or find my own. There were two girls who based their friendship on bribery and intimidation; one would always be waiting outside of the school doors with breakfast ready for the other to arrive, like a friendship servant. She'd shower her friend-servant with presents but was always expecting this intense loyalty in return. Years later I confronted them about their unhealthy friendship only to be told I was jealous, but I really wasn't; seeing their toxic friendship made me value my freedom. I bonded with a girl called Gemma as we both felt slightly out of our comfort zone at school but we were always in different classes, which meant we could only spend lunchtimes together and it stunted our friendship growth.

It was the first few years that were the hardest as I didn't have much confidence, but as the years went on I accepted the fact that I wouldn't have a solid group of friends at school like I was used to. Instead, I tried to get on with everyone and weave in and out of other groups. I wasn't the girl who sat alone at lunch, in fact anyone else at my school probably would have described me as quite popular, but I knew in my heart that I had few true friends there and so I just tried to get through it. Those childhood friendships were still strong outside of school but I wasn't convinced that I'd make any new friends and honestly, I didn't want to. My 'real' friends were at other schools making new ones and for the first time I felt really alone. This made me focus more on strengthening those childhood friendships, so I'd often skip any school social events on the weekend and see my non-school friends instead.

University posed a similar threat, which is why I never really wanted to go. When everyone else seemed desperate to get away from their home and throw themselves into student life, I saw it as another barrier where I would feel distant from my friends and family. After a careers teacher convinced me to apply, I got into the one university course that I applied for, making sure it was no longer than a two-hour drive from home so I could visit regularly. The majority of my university experience was really positive and it's where I started my blog and met my husband, but there's no doubt that my secondary school experience left me with a sour taste when it came to female friendships. I felt scarred from the negative experiences I'd been through and because of this I went through quite a few years of trying to avoid complicated female relationships by describing myself as a 'tomboy and definitely not a girl's girl', which now seems so ridiculous to me. Yes, I was always more into sports and less into handbags than the other girls, but it didn't make me any less of a girl's girl. I just felt let down and completely doubtful of the true meaning behind female friendships.

After a year living in halls we were able to choose who we lived with for second year, so I moved in with three boys and a girl who I got on really well with. The dynamic worked and we had a great year but throughout the year she had grown closer to some other girls and the boys had made other living arrangements for third year. I found myself at a bit of a loose end and I didn't want to miss out on a true university experience by living with my boyfriend. I was asked by a group of girls who I was friends with on my course if I wanted to join their new house plans and I was over the moon. Not only had I sorted living arrangements but I felt really included so things were definitely looking up. I asked if I could go and see the house with them, but they'd already done the first visit without me, so I asked if we could go again. When I went to the house, expecting us all to pick rooms out of a hat like we had done the year before, I was shown around with names pre-attached to each room. 'This is your room,' they said as I was shown to the only single bedroom in the house, a quarter the size of all the rest. Immediately those feelings of inclusion and comfort completely diminished; they only wanted me to fill the gap they needed in their living arrangements. I was gutted and felt really let down by the whole situation, it felt like school bullying all over again and I just wanted out. I had just enough confidence left to remove myself from the situation and make the decision to put myself first, but it completely changed my relationship with those girls for the last year of university. It sounds a bit dramatic now but during a time when I felt really homesick, it was crushing. I made less of an effort to win them over and focused my attention on my stud- ies, knowing I'd probably never see them again once the year was over. I moved in with two boys and it was the best decision; we're still close friends to this day and they were like my saviours during a time when I had little faith in female friendships.

It raised the question, how do you know if a friend is loyal? Can you ever predict these things and prevent them from happening? I think it takes personally experiencing a betrayal to know how to avoid it happening again and for a while it can make friend-making a very difficult task. How do you build up that trust again and know who to let in? Well, I guess you decide what's greater, the opportunity for a great friendship filled with love and companionship, or the potential threat of a let-down and disappointment. Do you jump in and risk the heartbreak that might never happen? Or do you stay safe but risk never experiencing true friendship-love?

There are a few signs to look out for and a few questions to ask yourself when you think a friendship is coming to an end . . .

- Has communication dropped off meaning you hardly ever speak anymore?
- Is one of you making all the effort and the other not giving anything in return?
- Have you started arguing more, getting really heated about topics that never used to be an issue?
- Are you growing in the same direction and changing at the same pace?
- Can you totally be yourself around them?

THE FRIENDSHIP HEARTBREAK TOOLKIT

A bottle of expensive red wine. Or maybe two. Fuck it, just get the one on offer!

Pizza. Always. And get the extra garlic-and-herb dip.

A trashy but brilliant film, preferably something starring either Drew Barrymore or Katherine Heigl.

A tub of Ben & Jerry's Phish Food, you know, the one with the chocolate fish in? There are two guys who'll never let you down.

A fluffy unicorn onesie made out of the most synthetic and sweaty material, BUT IT LOOKS COOL.

A charcoal face mask, because what's a stereotypical, emotional girl's night in alone without a really impractical, slightly painful face mask?!

FALLOUTS

We've all been there, no friendship is fallout-free. Whether it's a bicker that turns into a grudge and eventually gets forgotten about or a huge argument that ends a friendship entirely, we have definitely all been there. It's no secret that we surround ourselves with friends as some kind of self-validation. Friends are there to comfort, reassure, support and confirm things we know about life and we need them more than ever when things fall apart and our sense of self is challenged. When you fall out with a friend, you're suddenly faced with a lack of confidence and without the person you once trusted to turn to for advice; everything is questioned and it's hard to know how to move forward. The problem is, no matter how similar you think you are to your friends, ultimately everyone has different opinions. I personally find it quite difficult when I've had a disagreement with a friend and often have to ask someone neutral if I'm being unreasonable or if they are. You create a rule book in your head on how to be a good friend, so when someone does something that you deem to be against the rules, it's difficult to see it from their perspective.

A friend of mine once let me down, pulling out of an event that was important to me just a week before because of work. I personally thought her specific excuse wasn't good enough; had it been me, I would have stuck to my word and attended and I didn't feel like at the time she was apologetic enough. It took me by surprise and I didn't know how to handle it until I spoke to another friend, who reassured me that my feelings weren't completely irrational, but also helped me to see the other side of things and it helped me decide how I wanted to handle it. After bottling up my feelings for a while I decided it wasn't healthy to be angry without telling her how I felt, so I texted her and told her. I said that it wouldn't ruin our friendship and I wouldn't hold a grudge but that I wanted her to know how I felt and that I didn't agree with how she handled things.

It's difficult to have a clear perspective on a situation when you're so involved and in the heat of the moment you can say things you don't really mean. But how do you come back from stepping out of place? How do you forgive and forget if they crossed the line?

When you're in the wrong . . .

Apologise. Apologise. And apologise again. Know why you're saying sorry, mean it and show them how much you care. Don't expect them to forgive you straight away; say your bit and then allow them some space to think. But don't give up; if the friendship means enough to you then fight for it.

When they're in the wrong . . .

Decide how important the friendship is to you. Is it worth losing them over what happened? If they're completely unaware of how they upset you it's important to address it, but before you do, decide what you want the outcome to be. Go in with a calm temper, give them a chance to explain and then tell them how you would have preferred the situation to be dealt with. Then the important part is to let go . . . move on. If you want the friendship to work you have to learn how to forgive; holding grudges will only sour the relationship further.

When you're both in the wrong . . .

It usually takes a bit longer and another friend stuck in the middle to prove this one but it *can* happen. You're both right and you're both wrong in different ways – how are you going to solve this? Someone needs to make the first move and if you want to save the friendship, you might as well be that person. Really put yourself in their position and think of what you might have done wrong, address it and apologise but then let them know how they've upset you too, and try to find somewhere to meet in the middle.

When you discover you're wrong but it's gone too far . . .

Backtrack!! You may feel like it's gone too far, like there's no turning back, but a good friend will always be rooting for you and will accept an apology no matter how late it is. Better late than never!

When they won't forgive and forget . . .

So, you were in the wrong, you admit it, you've held your hands up and apologised profusely but they're having none of it. Let them know that you won't give up and stick to your word. They might not forgive you straight away and you shouldn't expect them to, but at every opportunity, without being suffocating, show them that you care about the friendship. Check in on them without putting pressure on them to forgive, remember you were the one in the wrong so don't put this on them to fix, always make sure you're taking the responsibility.

If you have a group of girlfriends rather than lots of separate friends, it's likely that at some point you might find yourself right in the middle of an argument between two friends. It's never your fault; something will happen, two friends will argue and then right when you think you're in the clear they say 'Well, what do you think?' . . . *and you're in.* My advice? Stay calm and follow the rules below.

- Speak to them both separately first to show you care for both of them
- Don't take sides, your opinion will only complicate things
- Listen to their side of things and clarify any rumours you know to be untrue
- Do not pass on information from one to the other
- Tell them you're there for them but you don't want to take sides or be involved
- Encourage each friend to think more about what they could have done differently instead of obsessing over the other's flaws
- Encourage each friend to focus less on the past and what's happened, and more on the future and how to move forward from it

Sometimes things can never go back to the way they were before the argument and in this case, the best thing to do is agree to disagree and to go your separate ways. You never know what the future holds and I believe that if it's meant to be, you'll find yourselves back on the same page, in a different stage of your lives, and you can pick up where you left off.

. . . the one who always feels left out

THE SENSITIVE FRIEND

You give a lot more thought to the sensitive friend. You add her birthday to your diary and repeat annually to make sure you *never* forget to buy her a card. You send her a text to invite her to join a gathering even if you know she's busy, because then you're covered in case she gets offended. You feel protective of her and although it can be more time-consuming to be her friend, you know she doesn't mean to be so sensitive; it's just how she is. She cries with happiness, like a bit too much, but she cries with sadness too. She makes you wonder if you're actually emotionless or if she's just overly emotional?! Whatever you do, DO NOT act offended by something she does or says because you will not hear the end of it, her guilt becomes your guilt and there are only so many times you can say, 'Really, I'm fine!' The sensitive friend sees rejection everywhere and can recall the friends who have shut her down in the past. You dread the day she has a break-up or gets into an argument with a mutual friend because there's no comforting her and honestly, seeing her heart-broken is heartbreaking for you. You wish you could take on some of her feelings so she doesn't have to deal with them all alone.

———

Do: *Accept her sensitivity and know it's more about herself than about you.*

Don't: *Let it consume you; it's not always your job to make her feel better.*

NO LONGER SINGLE & READY TO MINGLE

You know how we all have those friends who go from relationship to relationship, never really experiencing single life? Yeah, I'm that girl. I spent the years from 15 to 19 in two different long-term relationships before meeting my third at university. Fast-forward ten years and we're husband and wife, so my perspective on friendships has always been from a coupled-up point of view. I've had plenty of single friends, but I've never really *been* the single friend. I think because of this though, I have always been in very non-intense relationships and have never been in a 'we need some time alone' type couple. My relationships have always been based on being very sociable and inclusive and from the get-go I've always expressed how important my friends are to me.

My husband and I don't argue much, but it was whilst watching *Love Island* last summer (don't judge me) that I noticed he had been far too quiet through-out so I asked what was wrong. 'Finally, you've noticed that I haven't been speaking to you for the past 45 minutes.' *My bad.* It was then down to me to guess why he was annoyed. Floordrobe? Sofa-hogging? Hair in the shower? The potential list was endless, but it turned out that he was upset that when he asked me if I wanted to go away for our wedding anniversary, the first thing I did was check with my friend Anna that she didn't have any birthday plans that weekend that might clash. It's not to say that I wouldn't have gone if she had, but it was important for me to check and I didn't even think twice about it; that, for me, sums up how I feel about my friends. Finding a partner who was OK (most the time) with my friendship priorities meant a lot to me. 'It's one of your best qualities, but one of the most annoying for me,' he grunted.

There's no denying that when you first meet *the one*, step two is to get the approval from your mates. On a weekend trip back from uni, I sat in my parents' kitchen scrolling through Facebook trying to find the best photo of Rich to show off to Hannah. She's my 'older sister' friend, the one who helps me with my CV, the one who told me about the pill and the one who gives me all the life advice. It's a pretty pointless

exercise really because at this point when the excitement is so real, a good friend wouldn't dare say
anything other than 'FIT!' But that first approval
process has to happen, even if it's just to let you say
your thoughts out loud and confirm them with someone else. When and if things move on and become
more serious, that's when you *really* want the bonding
process to begin.

'*How did you know Rich would get on so well with
your friends?*' was one of those most asked questions
in an #AskLP Q&A video I did on my YouTube channel last year. It can be a real problem if your boyfriend
doesn't like your friends or vice versa so I wasn't
surprised to see the question pop up so many times.
Throughout all of my relationships, as far as I'm aware,
my friends haven't disliked the guys I've been with.
But are you ever really aware if they do? I've disliked
my friends' boyfriends in the past and only really ever
told them afterwards if they asked and genuinely
wanted to know. There's also a difference between
liking someone as a person and not liking how the
relationship works. I've often been in the position
where I think a friend's partner is probably a good
person but I just don't think they work particularly
well as a couple; that for some reason, whether it's

because they're too similar or too completely different, they don't bring out the best in each other.

So, let's start with the issue of when he doesn't like your friends, because somehow this one feels easier to manage. Maybe there's a clash of strong personalities, maybe he can't forgive them for how they once treated you in an argument or maybe he doesn't like what kind of friend they are to you. I've always been quite lucky as I've somehow ended up with a very laid-back, friendly husband who gets on with most people, but that's not to say he doesn't have his opinions or kick up a right fuss on the way to social situations. I think there are certain steps you can take to almost prep the introduction and I have found that really opening up and sharing with your partner how you feel about someone will help them understand the importance of the meeting. You've got all this knowledge inside you about how your friend is as a person; maybe she comes across as a bit rude when you first meet her but she's actually a real softie and her job is really interesting – share it! Tell him what to expect and tell him how important she is to you. It's natural for the bonding to take a little time and knowing when is the right time to bring them both together is key.

There are certain sociable friend situations that I

just wouldn't expect Rich to be on board with. So, a Sunday roast at the pub or a stroll through Broadway Market would be fine. But a takeaway and a bottle of wine surrounded by my girlfriends and me: not so fine. These women you've decided to surround yourself with were chosen by you, it's not fair to expect your partner to instantly feel the same way. There will be some friends of yours he likes more than others and having your own separate friends is also OK. Over the years it's become clear to me which friends of mine Rich really enjoys spending time with and which ones, although they get on, he has less in common with. I won't force him into every scenario; it's OK to see some friends alone, not everything has to be done in couples.

We all have the ability to get into very fiery arguments, but we are also able to reconcile those and move forward. It's often the case that, although all is forgotten between friends, loved ones can still feel the anger. How do you convince him to forgive and forget? I think this comes down to your relationship and the trust between you both; if you're open and honest with each other I think you can find a way to move forward without having to pick sides.

If you've noticed a friend is doing something to

make your partner feel uncomfortable or they clearly have a problem with him, I think it's up to you to take that upon yourself to address. If it's ignored and left up to him to address, it'll only cause problems in your relationship. As I said, I don't know much about when friends don't like your partner, but I do know how it feels when it's the other way around.

So, what if your friends don't like him? It's normal to want the best for a friend, but it's also normal to have different opinions on what exactly is best and this is usually where the problem arises. When it comes to love we're all looking for different things and it can be hard to understand when a friend is in a relationship that you don't agree with. Maybe he doesn't treat her like you think he should because he always cancels on her last minute, or he goes out of his way to embarrass her at the dinner table and it makes you feel uncomfortable to witness it. Or you don't understand how she can be attracted to someone with his personality traits; maybe he's lazy, messy, argumentative with everyone or makes inappropriate jokes that only she laughs at. If he shows no interest in getting to know you as the best friend and makes zero effort, it can make you feel unimportant and you wonder why she doesn't care more.

My friend Debs was in a toxic relationship that started in her late teens and ended in her early twenties. I never really liked him but I struggled to pinpoint why specifically, so I never mentioned it. The thing is, as the friend, it can feel too risky to say anything; I didn't want to hurt her feelings or risk losing a best friend. I remember just finding their relationship weird; for example, they never went on holidays together even though I knew she wanted to – she'd make up strange excuses for him, like he didn't like the sun. I was off at uni during this time so I used it as an excuse to let her figure it out for herself, I didn't know how to handle the situation at all. Her other close friends spent more time with them as a couple and so they found it more frustrating to see her in such a toxic place, often breaking down and crying about the relationship. A few years into the relationship they confronted her after hearing rumours (which were actually never proven) that he'd cheated and it was then that they all took the opportunity to tell Debs honestly what they thought of him. She was in such a bad place and we were worried that she was maybe being manipulated by him so that she misread their concern and chose to believe him and his convincing lies. It completely changed things between her and her friends because she was angry at them, she'd become so insecure and didn't think she could ever find love elsewhere so she couldn't understand why they'd threaten her relationship. It took her meeting some-one new to realise how damaging the relationship was and her friends stuck with her the entire time, forgiving her, comforting her and understanding the reasons why she chose him.

Even knowing how that story ended, I'm still not sure I'd have the guts to tell a friend that I disapproved of her romantic relationship. I value my friendships so much that the idea of risking losing one terrifies me; I guess that makes me a friendship coward. My angle is usually to try to get them to open up to me first so I can give some advice and make them realise in their own way that it's not good for them. I'll ask thought-provoking questions but try not to give too much of my own opinion or judgement. What is important is to prioritise and, as a good friend, the priority should be that they're happy in their relationship and to be there as a good friend to listen and advise if they're not. Making it all about you will only distance you further; as a friend, your job is to be there no matter what. I've had years of biting my tongue before witnessing a break-up and, without a doubt, the friendship comes out stronger if you're not the *I told you so* friend. But of course, it doesn't always end that way and you can't pin all your hopes on a break-up. If you want your friendship to work you have to embrace their decision to stay in their relationship and learn to be happy for them, even if you think it's the wrong decision. Confronting a friend about the doubts you have with their romantic relationship is a very risky game, because honestly, although we hope that friendship is as important as romance, it's not always that black and white.

The fantasy of true love and the idea of 'happily ever after' can often blind us and result in some bad decision-making. Some may think that a true friend will always be there for you and to risk losing out on love can feel far greater. As I've said, confronting a friend with your concerns about their relationship is risky, and I think if you simply don't like him, then don't do it. But if I truly felt that my friend was unhappy in her relationship but for some reason was unable to act upon it or felt trapped, or if I knew for a fact that they were in a dishonest relationship, I would then feel it right to speak to her. I would let her know that I was only concerned for her happiness and I was there for support and not to be judgemental. I think at this point your opinion of their partner is irrelevant; they're not asking you to date them, so unless you're asked, keep your comments to yourself. When friends start coupling up, it can really complicate a female friendship group and completely change the dynamic.

... *the one who always wants to go out*

THE SINGLE FRIEND

The single friend is always up for a fun night out but tell her you want to stay in with a curry and watch *X Factor* and she'll roll her eyes and tell you you're boring. She's been single for a while and you've tried to set her up a few times but she's *really* fussy . . .

The single friend would HATE the way you've just described her!

She's not the one to talk to about how much you're in love but she is genuinely happy for you (especially if he has some single mates). She'll be the last one to arrive at a friend's baby shower with the most stylish but inappropriate gift and labels herself as 'the cool auntie'. Don't ask her how her love life is going, she hates that question, but be prepared for her to launch into full detail about her most recent sexual escapade at any given time. You find yourself adding 'but we're really not coupley' onto the end of a dinner party invitation, and don't even bother with the New Year's Eve invite, she stays well clear of any smoochy New Year couples. You know deep down she really would like to fall in love, but what's great about the single friend is, even if she hasn't yet found love, she's always there to support you through yours.

––––––––––

Do: *Treat her the same way you'd treat your non-single friends.*

Don't: *Ask her how her love life is every time you see her.*

I think the time comes for us all, usually in our twenties, when an unspoken divide appears between single and non-single friends. Those who are single might resent their friend for wanting to stay in on a Saturday night and those coupled up might assume the other won't want to join in because they're single. It can be a real defining moment in a female friendship and how you deal with the change of dynamics can make or break it. As the girl who's always been in a relationship I think it's important to always be in tune with your single friend's life and where they're at. If you feel like you've let them down a few times and cancelled plans because all you really want to do is stay in and chill, make a real effort to balance that out. You might not want to spend time away from your partner but if you value the friendship you need to nurture it, and you'll appreciate it in the long run. It shouldn't be a waiting game where you're putting pressure on them to find someone so you can all hang out; integrate her into your couple life and make it less about who's in a relationship and who isn't.

HOW TO BE A GOOD NON-SINGLE FRIEND

- Don't try to set them up unless they actually want to be
- Don't assume they're unhappy just because they're single
- Don't define them by their relationship status
- Don't leave them out of social situations just because they're not in a couple
- Celebrate their successes even if it's not to do with engagements, babies or weddings

HOW TO BE A GOOD SINGLE FRIEND

- Don't assume that because she has a boyfriend she no longer wants to hang out and have fun
- Take an interest in her new relationship and get to know him
- Be happy for her; it shouldn't be a competition
- Being third wheel isn't always a bad thing; don't make it a bigger deal than it is and just enjoy hanging out
- Don't label her 'boring' because she is in the honeymoon stage and wants to enjoy spending time with him

When there begins to feel like a divide between single and non-single friends, it often gives an excuse to make some more friends, giving yourself the option of who to hang out with depending on the situation. But making new friends is easier said than done.

WILL YOU BE MY FRIEND?

Making new friends as an adult is hard and it's something we all struggle with, whether you're in your early twenties after university, mid-thirties and struggling to keep all your friends moving at the same pace, or in your fifties when the kids have moved out and you have more free time to play with. It's normal to feel like, that's it, you've missed your chance to make any new friends, but I refuse to believe that's true. As we get older and the idea of new friendships seems less accessible, we need to start looking for friendship in new and less obvious places. There are so many different ways to make new friends, it's just about embracing the opportunities that come your way and fighting against the natural anxiety that we as adults can associate with making friends.

As a kid, it's easy, you're placed in an environment that constantly encourages you to socialise and the relationships you form are nurtured with the help of those around you. Having just the smallest thing in common can give you enough of a reason to become the closest of friends. You want to be in the green scrunchie crew? *Get yourself a green scrunchie, girl. You're in!* But as adults, we have to make it happen ourselves. There are no teachers or structures around to encourage us to make friends. Our parents are far more concerned about who we're dating than who we're friends with, and our lives are already so consumed by work and keeping up appearances that making time to pursue new friendships is often dropped to the bottom of the priority list. As grown-ups, we over-think things and we fear the unknown; a lot of this stems from our fear of rejection and we let that fear hold us back because putting yourself out there is scary.

When making a friend we expose our true personality to someone new and with that comes the hope that they'll understand us, but this is a risk and our natural instinct is to protect ourselves from pain. This has been further complicated by the new wave of making friends online. It's easy to sit behind a computer, retyping a joke five times before posting it, whereas in real life there are no edits, filters or backspace buttons

– your most authentic self is all you've got to work with. Maybe you don't know where to look for new friends or how to make the first move, but we need to learn to overcome our fears and see it as a really positive experience and something to look forward to.

Let's be clear, I'm no friend collector. I realised early on in my life that having the wrong type of friend isn't beneficial to either of us and I've also learnt to have the confidence to know which friendships to pursue. As adults, we think more carefully about what a new relationship can bring to our life and whether a person has the right friendship style for us. For example, maybe the friendship style you feel most comfortable with offering is the role of 'the older sister friend', but then you might meet someone new who offers *you* support and advice and listens to *your* problems. Turns out they're the perfect new addition to your finely curated collection of friends and they bring more of a balance to the role you play within your friendships. Sometimes you can meet someone who has the wrong kind of friendship style and the expectations you have for the relationship don't match. For example, you might have a gut feeling that they'll take more from you than they'll give back and it's OK not to want to nurture that kind of relationship if you feel you already have a lot of friends like this. When making new friends you need to think about what's going on in your life and what's right for you at the time, whether you need a friend who will boost your spirits and bring about those high energy levels that you're craving, or someone who will sit and listen to you talk about your First-World problems with no judgement.

As grown-ups, we have the ability to be selfish and knowing what makes you feel good is key to knowing *who* makes you feel good. I'm more self-aware now than I've ever been; I know what makes me a good friend and I know my personality flaws and when I spend time with a new person I try to think about whether they bring out the best in me.

FINDING FRIENDSHIPS IN UNLIKELY PLACES

I asked a group of girls: 'When was the last time you made a new friend?'

- My boyfriend's mate's new girlfriend
- At work
- At a networking event
- At a hen party

- In a hostel when travelling
- At a festival
- At a local running club
- In a tour bus when travelling
- At a party
- Swimming the Channel
- Completely by accident when I knocked on the wrong house
- At a dog shelter

My friend Debs is great at making new friends; I think it's because she's open to the idea of meeting new people and it comes across to those who have encounters with her. Once, when she was in her late teens, she found herself tearful in the female toilets of a club after arguing with her (then) boyfriend. *Toxic guy.* On a boozy night out, the female toilets are Bonding Central, whether it's borrowing dry shampoo, passing toilet paper under the door or being asked, 'I love your top, where's it from?' She was comforted by another girl who asked if she was OK, and instead of brushing her off, Debs let her in, embraced her comfort and told her why she was upset. They instantly bonded and after a visit to the bar, she completely turned her night around; they shared a dance, laughed and at the end of the night exchanged numbers with the offer: 'If you ever need to talk . . . ' If Debs had replied, 'I'm fine, thanks,' it would have been a very different and lonely night. Sometimes these friendships are fleeting and don't turn into anything because they were perfect in that moment but realistically wouldn't work out as long-term friendships. But unless you open your eyes to the opportunities and embrace them, you'll never know. A new friend is always just around the corner . . .

. . . the one you have nothing in common with

THE HOLIDAY FRIEND

The holiday friend is one born from excitement, spare time and an unusual sun-induced sense of positivity. You find almost anything to bond over, whether it's matching bikinis, the same drinks order or your home country, *'OMG you're English?!'* The friendship goes from 1 to 100 in minutes as you make joint dinner plans, because dinner for four is way more fun than dinner for two. And let's be frank, none of your home friends are around to drive any competition! You can chat about the most random of topics because although you may exchange numbers or add each other on Facebook, deep down you know you'll probably never speak again. You pine for them in your post-holiday blues and refer to them in the weeks that follow as your friends roll their eyes and wait for the friend crush to pass . . .

Do: *Use this as an opportunity to test your own friend-making abilities.*

Don't: *Ruin the fun by actually trying to make the friendship work post-holiday.*

I hear the phrase 'a girl's girl' used a lot, often when someone is describing someone they've only just met. I was at a dinner recently and someone was gushing about a new friend, 'You know, she's just a real girl's girl.' Although I knew how *I* defined one, I asked her what she meant, just to clarify the reasons why she had that first impression. 'You know, the girl who is warm and friendly, who will compliment your hair and *actually* mean it. If you're walking out of the bathroom with toilet paper stuck to your shoe, she'll do everything in her power to catch you before you walk out, saving you from any embarrassment.' But are girls really so split down the middle? A girl's girl and . . . a guy's girl? When we spoke about the female who *isn't* a girl's girl we described someone who looks you up and down to judge you on your appearance, or someone who puts down everything you say with a competitive sting.

These are two very contrasting types of women – one who sounds lovely, someone you'd love to be friends with, and the other who seems like the type you'd want to avoid. But can you be somewhere in the middle, someone who's not a girl's girl but is still a decent person? I think you can. I know quite a few people who would always just prefer to spend time with their partner than with other females and in a way, they're not a typical girl's girl. I know someone who, although she has lots of female friends, was actually nervous to go on her own hen party because she just feels less comfortable around other girls. Some women believe that their boyfriend or husband can be their best friend, whereas I think a girl's girl would disagree with that. It's something I see quite often especially on social media, 'I'm so lucky to be marrying my best friend,' but I question whether a BFF is something we all look for in a partner or if it's healthier to keep love and friendships separate? For me the answer is simple; a group of friends, each of whom you go to for different things, is so important and I couldn't even imagine the pressure that would be put upon my husband if he had to be my 'everything in one'. The female friendships I have outside of my marriage mean that we can be husband and wife who, yes of course, know each other better than anyone else, but who don't *have* to be best friends. I even encourage Rich to speak to his friends, whether they're female or male, about certain topics I'm not confident in so that he can get an alternative opinion to my own. I don't like the idea of us being in our own separate bubble where we don't need anyone else; to me that's just not how life works.

If you're reading this thinking 'My husband is my best friend and I like it that way,' then don't fix what ain't broke, but if you do wish you had more female friends, it's never too late. I think that even if you're fundamentally not a girl's girl, you can still learn to be one. You can think about what you would look for in a girl you've just met, what first impressions would make you feel good, and then focus on doing those yourself. I think often shyness can come off as stand-offishness, even when it's not intended. I've met girls in the past who I had thought were quite rude, only to later find out they feel really awkward in social situations. So yet again, it can often be about working on yourself but also allowing potential new friends to help you improve. It only takes a connection with one person to give you a boost and a bit of confidence when you feel uncomfortable making new friends.

I never really considered you could be *too* good at making friends, but if I was to critique my sister Jojo in any way, it would be for that reason. It's kind of a nice problem to have really and it's what makes her such a warm person. If she gets a good vibe from someone she is very quick to embrace them; she'll be really open and honest, sharing tips and advice, inviting them over for a cup of tea and whenever people meet her they always say how nice she is. She's very good at making people feel at ease and she's *very* maternal, which is a trait that definitely makes people feel comfortable and safe when they're around her. This is why she often attracts quite needy people who lean on her for support and she's always happy to be there for them no matter how little she knows them, so they'll become really close very quickly. But what often ends up happening, and it's more since having kids and meeting new mum friends, is when the friendship develops and she finds herself in a situation where she needs to lean on them for support, they don't know how to be that friend to her.

You see, when you meet people after all your big life milestones have already happened, you can almost choose what to share and what not to share. So, unlike childhood friends, whom you've experienced everything with, you don't really know these new friends at all. For Jojo, all of a sudden, it's like she doesn't even really know that person and she's spent so much time being a good friend to them, she hasn't noticed that they're not right for her. I would say I'm quite picky when it comes to making friends; I'll be friendly to new people but I won't embrace them as a friend unless I really think they'll add to my life, and maybe this is because I haven't yet had kids and *had* to make these new friendships so often. I think in a way Jojo is less selfish than me, she thinks more about what that new person needs, but then because of that she finds herself with the wrong friends and they can fizzle out quite easily. It's difficult to know when you meet someone new whether they have potential to be a great friend or not, and often it can just be a feeling that you get. I admire Jojo for always giving it a go; it's without a doubt better than never making new friends, but maybe we could all be a bit fussier when it comes to choosing who to surround ourselves with.

MAKING FRIENDS 9 TO 5

Sometimes when we meet new people we're blissfully unaware that they could become someone special in our lives. Initially we might meet someone and see the potential for sharing skills or using each other as stepping stones on the career ladder, but those meetings can sometimes turn into friendships. As someone who's very career-driven I often find myself gravitating towards women who are full of ideas, have a sense of power and are willing to indulge in observational chat. I am frequently buzzing and packed full of endorphins after meeting someone and discussing plans for our new genius app idea or gap-in-the-market online service. The meeting of two minds, two sets of ideas and two lots of enthusiasm is how most of my adult friendships have started. I think for a lot of women the workplace is the hub for their adult female friendships and it's unsurprising in this modern world where lots of us find ourselves spending more time at the office with colleagues than we do with family and friends. Time spent at home can simply consist of eating, sleeping and getting ready to go back to work, so developing relationships in the workplace is incredibly important for your mental well-being.

A friend of mine, Jess, told me an amazing story about how a friend she made at work changed everything. She and Sim were close friends; they started with the usual small talk at work but pretty quickly knew they'd get on really well and drinks after work became a more regular thing. Eventually they took their friendship to the next level, going on double dates with their boyfriends and seeing each other on weekends. Friends talk about their friends, so naturally Jess had heard all about Sim's friend Paulina who had recently broken up with her boyfriend. Sim was confiding in Jess on how to deal with the awkward situation when you're friends with both people and they break up, so she knew all about the situation.

It was later on in the year when Jess also broke up with her boyfriend and she met Paulina for the first time at Sim's Christmas party. They started talking, bonding over their recent break-ups, and they completely hit it off and spent the whole night chatting. Paulina was very confident and took charge of the whole situation, demanding they meet up again, so they exchanged numbers and she made a plan. At the time, she had a part-time job looking after puppies so Paulina invited Jess over to meet them and have a cup of tea – *I mean, talk about a good first friend date!* Jess was a little nervous to go, still not knowing much about Paulina, but she was so glad she did because again, they got on just as well as they had at the party. Now here's where I think Paulina went wrong . . . If I had been in Sim's position, I would have been more than happy for my friends to meet and then take things further in meeting up without me, but I think there's almost a rite of passage that should happen before seeing each other alone. I think the first meeting after the party should have been with Sim, too, as she's the friend in common and the reason they met. Once a friendship has developed I think it's OK to meet up alone, but it's not really fair to ditch the introducer straight away.

After the first date, Jess and Paulina became even closer and would go for drinks together, forming their own friendship and memories. As time went on, Sim and Paulina fell out and grew apart; Sim felt that Paulina was being too controlling and trying to worm her way into her life and her friends' lives. She was jealous; her two separate friends had become stronger friends with each other and she felt left out. What's even crazier about this story is that Jess decided one night to invite Paulina on a night out to set her up with her brother as she thought they'd get on. Fast-forward five years and they're married with a kid, so now they're not only friends but also sisters-in-law! She actually said it's quite different now and that they're definitely more sisters-in-law than friends and that's because she hears about Paulina through her brother, so they've become somewhat lazy with communication and it's definitely affected their close-ness as friends. Paulina and Sim speak again now but there always seems to be a bit of competitiveness over Jess, with both trying to prove to each other that they know her better or are more of a priority to her. You never know what these new friends can turn into, they could end up being family!

The workplace *can* be a great environment for making new friends, but if you struggle to do so it can also be quite a lonely place. Starting a new job can be daunting, even terrifying for some, but it just takes that one girl on your first day to show you how the coffee machine works to make you feel welcome. One of the central struggles we face with our friendships in modern-day life is making time for your friends and being consistent with catching up. The luxury of a work friend is that you're forced to spend an abun-dance of time together and the purpose of that time isn't to make friends, so the pressure is off. When you learn a little more about each other every day, the bond becomes stronger and you might find yourself with the most amazing work wife!

... *the one who keeps you sane*

THE WORK WIFE

You can be totally honest with your work wife; she's so removed from your home life that your 'other' friends are just like characters so you can be brutally honest and descriptive with your stories. She knows the role they all play in your life and acts as a great sounding board for when you're in a complicated situation. You've got a great work rhythm and the slight competitiveness between you is what encourages you both to keep pushing and succeeding within your roles. When it comes down to it you care enough about the friendship to put it first and you've crossed the line over to *real* friend so you know the friendship would continue if either of you moved on. She's the reason you don't dread going into the office and the comfort blanket you need on a cold, drizzly Monday morning. She will follow you into the bathroom when you've just had a disastrous, tear-inducing meeting and she's always on hand for a cup of tea and a debrief in the kitchen. You're from different worlds, and sometimes have completely different backgrounds, but your career goals match up and your shared drive and ambition is what binds you as close friends.

———————

Do: *Try to take it to the next level by meeting up outside of work.*

Don't: *Get into the habit of only talking about work when you're with her.*

If you're someone who has a lot of childhood friends, meeting people at work can be a really great way to connect with people who, although they don't know your past as well, probably 'get' you now a lot better than your older friends do. It can feel like a relief to have people around you who have similar career goals, salaries and day-to-day life routines. When I found myself interning at a beauty company I was so relieved to be working with a girl who, like me, also ran a blog as a hobby alongside her job. Zoe and I bonded immediately; she taught me so much about the beauty-blogging world, about how to improve the design of my blog, and she even took me to my very first blogging event. This was the first time I'd met anyone else who had a blog; none of my childhood friends were into it and so having someone at work I could connect with about something I was so passionate about was really exciting. Meeting Zoe and throwing myself into the beauty-blogging community really gave me the opportunity to meet so many new people with the same, quite niche, interests that I had.

I really thought by this point that my friend-making days were gone and I was happy with the close friends that I had, but at 25 years old I met my friend Anna, who, if you saw us together, you'd think I'd known my whole life. We'd both watched each other's videos online and read each other's blogs and gradually we started tweeting and interacting with each other's content. The first time we met was at a blogging event in early 2012; Zoe was launching her own lipstick, so we both went along to support her, and we excitedly hugged when we met because it felt like we'd known each other for years. I'd been working in my beauty PR and marketing role for about a year and Anna had an almost identical role at a competitor company. Our bosses prepped us both before the event, trying to convince us to find out information from the other, but what happened was quite the opposite. We spent the evening confiding in each other, bonding over the fact neither of us loved our jobs and gushing over how much we loved blogging and making videos on YouTube.

Unlike any of my other friends, Anna was in exactly the same place in her life as me, doing the same job, feeling the same way and although we came from different places and had different backgrounds we just *got* each other. It blew my mind that I could meet someone at 25 who was so similar to me, I remember even my friends being shocked and saying how perfect we were for each other. We spent the next eight months becoming really close friends; she'd come up on weekends and stay with me in London and I'd do the same, going to visit her in Brighton. We started going to blogging events after work together and our content began to cross over as we'd encourage one another to pursue our passions and film videos introducing our separate audiences to the other. In September that year it got to the point where I had become marketing manager at work but my blog and YouTube channel had become quite successful and I was spending every evening and weekend working on it. Anna and I had always discussed the possibility of blogging full-time but we didn't know many others who were doing it. At this point she was renting in London so quitting her job felt too daunting, but I was living at home and knew it was my only chance to give it a go.

I quit my job in October 2012 and a month later, after going part-time, Anna quit hers too. We pushed each other to risk it all, to pursue our passion, and we supported each other throughout the whole experience when our other friends and family thought we were mad. I'm not exaggerating when I say I think we've spoken almost every weekday since October 2012. I travel more with Anna than I do with my husband or family, which means she's seen me at my very worst; when I'm unwell, homesick, jetlagged or stressed.

Our friendship has been so intense and concentrated over the past five years that we've managed to create so many memories and funny stories that feel fresh in our minds. One time on a press trip in Stockholm we both took travel sickness pills before getting on a ferry to a very smart event, not realising they would make us incredibly drowsy. We spent the entire evening desperately trying to hold our eyelids open, using the singing performances between meals as an excuse to have a little nap whilst the lights were dimmed. Neither of us realised the other was feeling the same until the end of the night when we of course burst into hysterical, tired laughter realising what we had done. We excused ourselves from the party and it's fair to say no one else saw the funny side but we still crack up now thinking about it.

Spending so much time together means that we're often with each other when memorable life moments happen. I was with Anna when one of my closest friends called me to say she was engaged just as we were getting on a plane; we were together when I realised another friend had gone into labour, and she was also right beside me when I found out we'd had our offer accepted on a house, so it's fair to say we've seen each other cry on multiple occasions. It's usually on a plane – they say your emotions are heightened up there. For me, reading *The Fault in Our Stars* set me off, and for her it was watching *Lion*. Oh yes, we've seen each other's ugly crying faces plenty of times. We've shared many hotel rooms over the years; she knows to play music when I go to the toilet so I don't get stage fright and I know she'll probably wake up topless because she de-layers in her sleep. She's the tidy one who unpacks and fills the wardrobe neatly, I try desperately not to upset her Virgo ways by using the chair in the corner to throw my clothes on instead of doing a complete 'floordrobe'.

More than any of my other friends, Anna and I have roles within our friendship that are clearly defined and that we stick to. She's always the navigator when we go places, mapping out the route and getting us there safely, but I'll pick the restaurant and if something is wrong with her meal, I'll complain to the waiter for her. I'll also make her try my meal if it's something she's never tried before – I like to make her try new things and I think that's what works really well about our friendship. We're very similar in some ways but also very different in others. She teaches me how to be calmer and more organised, and she'll always have a very fair, level-headed opinion on things and I think I teach her how to be more spontaneous, confident and sometimes I'll push her to be more selfish and to prioritise herself. I think anyone who has a job that's maybe a little out of the ordinary will relate when I say that sometimes it's easier not to talk about work to friends. I try to be as open as I can with my friends but often indulging in my worries or stresses can be impossible for them to relate to and I end up having to explain myself to the point where I wish I hadn't brought it up. It's comforting knowing that I can speak to my work wife at any point and she'll totally get what I mean without any explanation, and it means I can spend time with my other friends without much work chat and without needing them for that kind of support.

We crossed the line from colleagues to close friends pretty quickly, which means now we have the best of both worlds. We can hang out on the weekends and not even mention work, but we can also speak in the week and indulge in our worries, both sharing advice. I think that's how you turn a work friend into a week-end friend too, by opening up and speaking to them about non-work topics. It's that moment where you introduce them to your out-of-work friends or they meet your family at your birthday; that's when you know you're becoming 'real' friends. It feels different, too; you know that you can totally be yourself in front of them and you can sit in complete silence without having to fill the space with small talk.

It must depend on your job, but for me, my work wife is *so* important that I'm not entirely sure I'd still be doing my job without her by my side. I thought my best friends were set in stone but meeting her completely threw me, because here's the thing: there's always room for another best friend. I often get teased for using the word too loosely and I *know* it defeats the meaning of 'best', but I really do have a few and I'm one lucky lady. You never know when or where you might meet someone who slots right in, there are so many different women in this world – over three billion in fact! Each is unique and each can bring something entirely new and different to our lives.

ALL THE FRIENDLY FISH IN THE SEA: HOW WE CAN TURN E-FRIENDS INTO REAL FRIENDS

Social media has opened up a whole new world when it comes to the potential for new friendships. Our entire lives we were told never to talk to strangers but in some small twist of fate, the Internet brought about exactly that. For the first time ever we were connecting with strangers around the world and the link was often a shared interest, because humans are tribal and like to be surrounded by like-minded people. Social media enabled us to build and curate a new network for ourselves but it can sometimes be difficult to turn these online connections into real-life friendships. We spend every day with these people. They know where our offices are, what we had for breakfast and what we're reading for our book club; their insight into our lives is uncanny and they often know more about our quotidian likes and dislikes than our besties or even our own mothers.

... the one who you chat to in 140 characters (or 280!)

THE ONLINE FRIEND

The online friend is the one whose friendship is purely online. You followed her first and started liking her photos, 'favouriting' her tweets, and then she started to follow you back. *OMG! *Thinks very carefully about all future tweets.** She is *hilarious* and manages to observe and share the sort of awkward social situations you can totally relate to. Are you the same person?! You find yourself referring to her too often and your actual friends find it weird that you've never even met the girl – you know you'd get on like a house on fire if you did. Occasionally you'll DM each other, which makes you feel like you're sort of *real* friends. Maybe it would ruin the mystery if you met? The fantasy of the friendship is far too good to risk losing. Her bio pic is so familiar to you that if she walked past you in the street it would be like bumping into an old friend.

Do: *Remember to check in every now and again, don't be tempted to silently stalk!*

Don't: *Obsess over how long she takes to reply or if she likes as many photos of yours as you do of hers.*

So, is it possible to make these e-friends turn into real friends? There's that girl on Twitter who posts the most hilarious GIFs and every now and again you have a GIF-off, bonding over your mutual love for *Parks and Recreation*. You want to take things to the next level but the Twitter friendship is very public. Your conversations connect on a consistent thread that can be seen and read by all of your followers, so you think about everything you're saying in a very intense and microscopic way. After all, you've only got 280 characters with which to woo and entertain your e-mate – *talk about pressure!* Twitter is a great tool for friendship flirting, you can do the odd like or retweet here and there without ever really going into a deeper conversation, but it's hard to move beyond that.

Then there's the girl on Instagram who you've been following for months – you know the layout of her living room, her favourite spot in the city for taking an outfit pic and her favourite brand when it comes to athleisure – you've mutually liked each other's photos but never gone as far as commenting. Instagram is a weird social space when it comes to making friends because it's inspiring and intimidating in equal measure. With 68% of Instagram users being female, a lot of women follow other women and whilst this creates aspiration – which is good – it also has us doubting our own lifestyles. For this reason, it can be a difficult place to make a friend.

So, what's the next move? It takes just one person to put themselves out there and slide into the DM. There's really only so much top-line chat that can be had publically, but direct messaging is where the real magic happens. A private corner of the Internet for a two-way chat, there's no end goal, time pressure or public scrutiny and with the pressure off you can have a more real and honest conversation. Is there anything more fulfilling than opening up your Instagram and seeing that little red '1' pop up on the top right-hand side? You realise the girl you've been crushing on is following you back and now she's sliding into your DMs. It's that feeling you get when your 13-year-old self gets a text from the boy you fancy. It's taking the relationship to the next level and all of a sudden you feel important, noticed and you can go deeper with your chat. DMs allow you to open up and share more of your personality, which in turn will allow them to trust you and do the same.

With the rise of social media, the Internet has inspired more and more in-store meet-ups, workshops and blogger events that bring women who have connected online together into a real space. Brands are giving more power to the average consumer and they now know the importance of connectivity and getting women in a room together. Nike and their women's running club is a great example of this as well as Stylist Live, a 'festival of inspiration'. Over the years I've hosted multiple events of my own and I'm always amazed by how many people are willing to put themselves out there and turn up without knowing anyone else. Seeing the women at my events connect and make friends brings me so much joy and when they come back to the next event together as *real life* friends, it reminds me how beneficial it can be to just turn up and give it a go.

Social media has its own slightly terrifying way of grouping us together, introducing us to other like-minded people and encouraging us to connect with those we might have something in common with. It just takes confidence and courage to reach out and take the online friendship offline and into the real world. The vast majority of people you'll interact with on social media will be sincere and honest in the information they provide and their reasons for using the platform. However, there are exceptions, and it's incredibly important to stay safe online.

THE E-FRIEND MEET UP

'Hey! Hope you're well? This is a bit random but fancy meeting up for a drink? Would be great to finally meet you & catch up! Xx'

'OMG yes, I would love that! Where do you fancy going? I can do after work on Wednesday? Xx'

'Anywhere with wine! Can't wait to meet you! Xx'

'Perfect, send me an address and I'm there! X'

Whether it started online or offline, you've made plans to meet up, now what? The initial meeting might be nerve-wracking but have some topics in mind to discuss and BE A GOOD LISTENER. No one is a fan of small talk and my tip for getting around it is to make an effort, really listen and show an interest in the conversation. When you ask them about their job don't reply with 'Cool,' reply with another relevant question to learn more about their role and what it is they like about their job. It makes people feel good when others show genuine interest in them and this will help put your new friend at ease. It seems so obvious but you have the power to lead the conversation if you want to, and if they're not asking you enough questions then offer up your answers anyway. It's OK to say: 'I'm going to the theatre tonight to see *Les Misérables*, have you seen it?' It's OK to force conversation starters; if anything, the other person will appreciate your efforts. The people who stand out to me are the ones who take a real interest in whatever we're discussing and make proper eye contact with me. There's nothing worse than talking to someone who's looking around for someone better to talk to. But taking control of a conversation takes confidence and it's a skill that can be developed over time; for me it's actually something I've learnt from meeting my viewers over the years. Knowing the right questions to ask and being able to listen and guide the conversation is a really useful skill when making new friends.

Seems easy, right? But then what if it is just awkward? What if you have nothing to chat about and you run out of things to say? My advice on this would be that you have to take a risk – you might just find yourself non-stop chatting, not realising where the time has gone because you're *so* on the same page and have *so* much in common. But also, if you don't, that's OK too. Perhaps your online personas look like they'd make for great friends but in real life there's no chemistry. It's just like going on a romantic date and if there's no spark, that's OK, you've not lost anything more than an hour of your time in a cafe. Sometimes it's a good thing to recognise when a friendship isn't a natural fit and you don't need to force it. In the past, I've been offended and have experienced feelings of insecurity when I've pursued a friendship and not got the same level of effort back. Now I can see that without the joint effort it wouldn't have been a healthy friendship anyway. I try not to let myself get paranoid about the reasons some people might not want to become a friend of mine because everyone has different qualities that they look for in a friend and you can't expect everyone to love you. Move on, there are plenty of other friendly fish in the sea!

Sometimes friend dating is about the experience, and when meeting new people, you'll learn more about yourself throughout the process. This will only benefit you the next time you try and make a new friend. For example, I sometimes find when I'm around certain people I become really negative and almost shut down their positivity. As a natural pessimist, I know I have it in me, but when I'm around the right people it doesn't show as much and I can tap into the more positive side of my personality. Occasionally, I'll leave a social situation thinking, for whatever reason, that person didn't bring out the best in me and that's not the person I want to be.

I was once sat next to someone at a wedding who seemed really friendly and we started with the usual 'What do you do?', standard boring wedding-guest chat, and so I told her what I did for work. With a job like mine it always gets a slightly different reaction but hers was instantly snooty; she was one of those people who would call Art A level a 'Mickey Mouse subject'. She fired some questions at me, all with a negative angle, like she was almost answering them herself. 'Is it a struggle to make good money?', 'You must get lots of hate, right?', 'I wish I could quit my day job and just have fun all day like you.' Her attitude and the atmosphere she created made me become this over-the-top show-off, desperately trying to prove my worth and prove to her that I worked hard to get where I was. I think at one point I referred to myself as an 'influencer', which is something I would *never* do, I hate that word!

I spent the entire rest of the evening just thinking 'I hate that woman!', but mainly because she made me hate myself and the way I was acting. She brought out the very worst in me to the point where I didn't recognise myself and I spent so long reflecting on how I wished I'd reacted instead. Why did I allow her to aggravate me, instead of just accepting that we were very different and finding someone else more interesting to talk to? Luckily, we never had to see each other again but had that been a friend date, it would have been a disastrous one. Sometimes it's clear straight away if a friendship won't work and sometimes it requires a little more investigating . . .

Any friendship requires time and effort to bloom into something special, whether online or offline. When the world of social media first launched, the idea of sharing my thoughts and opinions to complete strangers all over the world didn't make any sense to me. I'm pretty sure my first ever tweet was 'Lily Pebbles has been forced to join Twitter', grumpy AF. Over the years, though, the way I feel about social media has completely changed and I have to admit it is a great way to meet new like-minded people. I was in the friend comfort zone hanging out with the same people time and time again, but being online has exposed me to different women from completely different backgrounds who happen to share my interests and passions. Sometimes I think about how many people there must be just in my city alone who I would get on and enjoy being friends with; it's exciting knowing that you can continue to keep making new friends throughout your life.

When it comes to friendship, the world of tech is more on board than ever before. When they say there's an app for everything they're not kidding, and friendship is no exception. Cliq is a 'social discovery' app that allows you to meet new people based on your location. You can swipe through profiles, adding anyone of interest to your group so you can all chat together before it automatically deletes the messages 24 hours later. Using your location, it'll suggest where to meet, or which activity to do together so you're all set for your friend date.

The dating app Bumble, where women have to make the first move, has now extended its services by creating Bumble BFF, a way to meet like-minded women. They found that those who had found love were keeping the app on their phone, changing their 'interest' to same-sex and using it to find new friends, so the idea for Bumble BFF actually came from the users themselves. Today there are apps for all kinds of friend-making: you can meet fellow sports lovers, dog owners and some apps even enable you to make friends together with your existing friends, like group dating.

Meet My Dog is one that connects you with other local dog owners in your area; it allows you to set up play dates at your local park and hang out with a new fluffy friend (and their owner, who you might like too!) One of my personal favourites, because I think it's one that is so necessary, is Peanut – tagline 'Meet as Mamas, Connect as Women'. At a time when you can feel quite lonely, a bit like you've lost your former self, Peanut brings together 'women who also happen to be mamas' and allows them to chat and form a supportive community.

Twitter hashtags have also become a great way of finding new people with similar interests; they group together a topic so you can see the whole conversation in one place. Blogosphere, a quarterly magazine created for the blogging community, utilises this very well using the hashtag '#blogospherechat'. As well as weekly chats held at a specific time around a specific topic, the hashtag is continuously used by bloggers and those interested in blogging to share tips and ask questions. A well-run hashtag can be the perfect place to stumble upon an abundance of like-minded people discussing a topic that you feel passionate about. Social media is no longer just about watching cat videos or keeping up with your favourite Kardashian; the opportunity for actually making real friends online is greater now than ever.

I wanted to write about what it's like to actually use a friend dating app; I searched and searched for someone to tell me a story about their experience but couldn't find anyone. I toyed with the idea of trying it out myself but then quickly shut it down thinking, *No way, how cringe!* But then how can I recommend trying it if I'm too much of a coward to do it myself? So, one night I grabbed my phone and downloaded Bumble BFF; I'd seen an ad for it on the side of a black cab and the girls they used in the campaign looked nice. I signed in, connected with my Facebook page, opted for the BFF feature (you can also look for love or business networking) and then started to build my profile. I added a description about myself, *I'm always terrible at these,* 'Hi, I'm Lily! I'm creative, I love photography, style, beauty & discovering new places to eat in London. Yes that's me dressed as a giant boob'. I had to scroll through the photos on my phone, desperately trying to find some that I thought made me look friendly, kind and not like a poser, which is hard when you're a blogger who's had eight years of OOTD (outfit of the day) practice. I uploaded four, one of me on holiday, one of me holding my camera (got to show off those hobbies!), a posy one in New York (idiot) and one of me dressed as a giant boob for charity. *I wouldn't want to date me.* Job description? *Oh God.* They actually have the option for blogger, which is exciting but again, I'm not entirely sure that's an approachable, non-intimidating job title. OK, so I've built my profile, I'm mortified at how cringeworthy it is and now I guess I have to make friends?

It takes me onto a page with a large photo of someone I don't know; it says at the bottom, 'Brianna, 35, Administrative Assistant,' and then the university she attended. She looks fun, she's at a festival with face paint on. *Oh God, my photo is far too professional.* But maybe she's too fun for me? I want someone I can meet for tea, not shots. *This is MAD, I didn't realise how nervous I'd be.* I swish her photo to the side and go onto the next. 'Sophia, 30, Marketing Manager.' *Ooh, she looks nice!* I'm 30 and I work in marketing, kind of. She has a friendly face, she's smiling and in her photo, she has a bottle of wine and she's on a boat, which makes me think she's fun but in a grown-up way. She went to uni in America . . . *Ooh, there are more photos if I scroll down.* She's travelled, somewhere with a waterfall, she has a boyfriend she wants to show off and her bio says she's new to London, she's a feminist, she's a loud laugher and a proud cat mum. *I'm not sure. I'm going to swipe on. This is strangely addictive.*

OK, just checking in, I've been sat here scrolling for about fifteen minutes. It's harder than you think, I guess usually you don't judge a potential new friend based on a static photo, a short bio and a job title. Also, the fear of what happens when you swipe right got real, but I finally did it. I found a girl who I think I'd get on with, she's a bit younger than me but she's added her Instagram handle, which meant I could do some stalking. She uses the same Fujifilm camera that I love so we'd be able to chat about that and I can see from her profile that she loves travelling and taking beautiful photos when she does. I think she'd get my job and find it interesting, I wish I could tell you what she does but now I've swiped right she seems to have disappeared from my life. I think what happens now is that I have to wait to see if she picks me too because unless we match, we can't chat. *I've never been so nervous in my life.*

Whilst I wait I continue to flick through and find a few more ladies who look nice; one is looking for someone to have brunch with; *I like brunch!* I've definitely noticed that there's a trend of girls who have just moved to London from abroad and are looking to build up a new circle of friends, although one girl quite honestly wrote that all her friends were settling down, getting married and having babies so she is looking for friends who still want to go out and party with her – *fair enough.* OK, I think I've swiped enough, it keeps asking me if I've made a mistake by swiping left – *does that mean I've done it too many times?* I'm going to close the app and come back to it later, let's see if anyone wants to be my friend . . .

OMG, I have a match. She's a teacher, the one who enjoys brunch! I've messaged her to say hi; apparently, she has 24 hours to respond. *Maybe I should have said something more interesting than 'Hi'?* She replies about an hour later saying, 'Hey Lily, how's your Tuesday going?' but now when I click on her it says 'deleted user' and I can't reply. *Was she a fake?* Why do I suddenly hear my dad's voice in my head telling me not to speak to strangers on the Internet . . .

About an hour later I get matched with another girl,

yay, the app asks if I want to make the first move. OK . . . I message her saying 'Hey Sara, hope are you?' and press send . . . *yep, you read correctly, I misspelt 'how' – great start, Lily!* But then she replied, it was all very exciting! We spent the evening chatting, it took me back to my MSN Messenger days but thankfully a/s/l is no longer a thing (age/sex/location, for those of you who didn't grow up in the 90s).

The conversation was flowing but then it just stopped . . . *maybe she'd gone to have dinner or to take out the washing?* I woke up the next morning and immediately checked the app to see if she had replied. *Nothing.* There was no way I could follow up my message, it was a question and I'd look so needy if I messaged without waiting for a reply. I went about my day as usual, checked it a few times, but I heard nothing. Three days passed and there was still no message. *Was that it? Had I been ghosted?* I genuinely thought we'd message for a few days then maybe meet up, isn't that how it works? Apparently not. Either she decided I wasn't her 'type' or she'd been distracted and forgot all about me; either way it was pretty crap for me. Our friendship was fleeting. *I can't really call it a friendship, can I?* I enjoyed our chat though, as short as it was, and now I've tried it, I would recommend an app for meeting people. Maybe Sara

Hey Sara! Hope are you?

So cringe!

Hey Lily!!
I am good just chilling at home :-) Oldschool emoji
How are you   – Interesting

I'm good thanks! Honestly I've never used a friend
making app before but thought I'd give it a go.
It's kind of terrifying but it's such a good idea

Trying to be honest + show vulnerability

It really is!! I used a social networking event thing
before when I moved to London and met a girl
from there we have been best friends for years now.
What do you blog about?

Is she hinting that
we could be best
friends one day

Showing interest, nice!

Ah that's so nice! Beauty, style... a bit of
everything really. What do do for work?

I shut this down too quickly. I got nervous!

Aw nice! I am a legal p.a so my job is boring compared
to yours! Are you originally from London?

Putting herself
down, I would have
preferred her to be
proud of her job

Ha. I'm sure it's not boring!
Everyone else's jobs always seem
more exciting. Yes, born here.
When did you move to London?

I moved here about ten years ago. I lived just
outside and used to commute into work. I lived with
my bf so when we split I just moved to London.

Opening up. Sharing personal stories

Do you like living here?

Maybe I should have shared something personal too

153

and I weren't destined for a lifetime of friendship but as I witnessed during my 15 mins of swiping, there are *plenty* more people out there wanting to make friends. I think for now I'll stick to the ones I have in real life, but I did have fun and it was nice to remember that exciting feeling you get when you meet someone new. Maybe one day I'll start up my account again, maybe next time with some slightly more approachable photos . . .

300 FRIENDS AND COUNTING: HOW SOCIAL MEDIA IMPACTS IRL FRIENDSHIPS

There are no 'dislike' buttons in real life. Often, if you don't like something, you walk away from it, or at worst, you bitch about it behind its back – writing a bad hotel review was about as confrontational as it got! Interestingly, Facebook recently removed the dislike feature, perhaps realising (a little bit too late maybe) that a network created for connecting people has the opportunity to shine a positive light on friendships. When Facebook launched I was 17, so I grew up in the Nokia 3210 era when a pixelated snake game was the most exciting thing you could hide from your teachers. I was in my final year of school and we'd use my friend's older sister's university email to log in and snoop around. There really wasn't much to do on there initially, but as a creative person, the idea of sharing photos really appealed to me.

Before Facebook we used MSN Messenger to chat to boys from school and we'd search frantically on local chat forums trying to find a glimpse of our names, only to be disappointed when what we found was a bitchy comment. I'll never get over reading the first nasty comment about me online: 'Lily's hair is so frizzy she looks like she's been electrocuted,' . . . cue hair complex and years of obsessive straightening. I never got into MySpace, I think I was a few years too old (and not quite emo enough) and so Facebook for me was the real start to the social media era.

If I'm honest, I think Facebook took the meaning of friends, turned it into a popularity contest and disguised it as 'connecting'. Don't get me wrong, I think it's genius and Facebook has *so* many positives, like reconnecting you with old friends, sharing your travel photos and stories with family and keeping you in contact with those living abroad. Let's not forget the ever-so-useful ability to 'poke' someone . . . *eyebrow raise.* But there's no denying how much the social network has changed friendships and I'm not entirely sure it's for the better. Initially, it was all about sending as many friend requests as possible, adding every person you'd ever met and getting the most likes on a photo or status update. 'Add me on Facebook' was the new 'What's your number?' and you'd wait apprehensively to see if your friend requests would be accepted so you could stalk to your heart's content. Eventually, you'd find yourself with 300 friends, only 40 of whom you'd say hi to if they walked past you on the street. Pretty quickly sharing it online became more important than the experience itself and liking a status made you look like a good friend. Why call her to see how she is if you've already seen all the 'sausages or legs' photos from her recent holiday and heard all the funny anecdotes in her daily status updates?

In the past, you would have sent a card to your loved one, but typing and posting 'happy birthday' on their wall became the replacement. Where you once might have phoned your friend to tell them about the crazy thing that just happened to you, posting it in a status and eagerly waiting for the likes to roll in became the norm. It all began to feel very detached and inhuman and as someone who grew up writing diaries I personally love a handwritten card and felt it was quite a sad transition. I think when I really noticed how tech had changed communication was when I received my first

Moonpig greeting card with preprinted text inside – it felt like anyone could have typed it. There's something so comforting about recognising the handwriting or nicknames in your birthday cards; my grandma always dates hers in the corner, Debs always signs off 'Danny' because of a silly childhood game we played and Gemma writes 'Dear Hot Sally' because of when she misread my furry pink 'Hot Stuff' sweatband I once wore as a teenager. I'm still not entirely sure why I wore a pink furry sweatband on my wrist that said 'Hot Stuff', but that's another story. Facebook launched and suddenly there was no more need for S.W.A.L.K. – you couldn't seal a Facebook message with a loving kiss.

But it seems now things have changed again, perhaps because we're more experienced when it comes to integrating social media into our friendships. At the beginning, everyone jumped on the bandwagon and got involved, not really knowing what to expect from it or what some of the ramifications might be. But then the Internet was tried and tested and people discovered what worked for them and what they didn't like about sharing their life online. There was no 'one size fits all' and over the years my friends and I have changed the way we interact on social media. At first it was all-consuming. We'd upload an endless number of photos to show off what we were up to, an event wouldn't exist unless it was sent via Facebook and we'd regularly write cute little messages on each other's walls. As time went on things changed, maybe some of us experienced negativity online or found ourselves feeling jealous over a situation you normally wouldn't think twice about. Whatever the reason, our individual opinions on sharing online began to develop; some would obsess over it, making three status updates a day, whilst others found it vain and would cringe at the thought of even having a profile photo. Some held back from sharing online and others deleted their profiles altogether and then it became an unreliable way to keep up with friends.

And this doesn't just apply to Facebook; after years of being *so* online it's become cool to be offline and to actually see your friends face to face. Sending a handwritten note or spending an evening with a friend and making a point of turning your phones off are the things that are becoming special and valued. Before social media, we used our mobiles for the odd call and text, so I never imagined a time when I'd be going out with my friends for a 'blackout dinner'. Gestures offline, to me, seem so thoughtful compared to the ease of an online message. Sending flowers to a friend just because you think they need cheering up after a busy week at work, buying a book and writing a message in the front page because you think they'll find it interesting, finding a funny old photo of when you were younger and sending it in an envelope with a message on the back – it's these moments that make us realise how much someone really cares.

THE BLACKOUT DINNER

All phones in the middle of the table, no selfies, no emails, no browsing on Instagram allowed. The first one to go for their phone pays for dinner. Social media *does* help us to connect, but sometimes, especially when it comes to maintaining friendships, it's really important to disconnect.

My most memorable experiences with friends are not those that were had on any social media platform, they're the face-to-face special moments that we've shared in real life. Social media is a huge part of my job, but in my mind, I've kept it quite separate from my real life. Everything I do and say online is honest and true but it's not the whole of me, it's just one curated aspect of my life and I keep parts of it back that I only share with friends and family. A few years ago, I started to realise that whilst I knew I was only sharing elements of my life through a certain lens, my friends didn't. And I found that gradually they were taking less and less interest in what I was up to. They wouldn't ask what I'd been doing, where I'd been or how work was going because they assumed that they had seen it all online already. I often need to remind my friends that what they see of me online isn't all of me. Although the line feels blurred at times, my job has made me value my friendships even more; it's made me closer to those I know I can open up to and trust. Putting my phone away and turning off my camera is something I'm very conscious of, as I think my friends deserve my full attention and I think it's really healthy to have boundaries.

MOVING AT A DIFFERENT PACE

For so long your life is moving at a pace that is set by education, but as you get older it's a bit of a free-for-all. It's like we're all heading in the same direction and then school ends and we all split off. I think the biggest change of pace my friends and I experienced was after school, with some of us giving university a go and others choosing not to. I remember feeling quite envious of a friend who chose not to go and instead started working in fashion; she was earning decent money whilst I was living the student life eating baked beans on toast and staying up all night to reach deadlines. But then maybe she felt envious of how much fun I was having and the new friends I was making? I'd go home quite a lot and we'd catch up then, but during those three years she only came to visit me once so we mainly stayed in touch through social media and texting. Our lives were in such different places throughout those years that it's almost like we pressed 'pause' on our friendship and then picked it straight back up when I finished. I think it's a true testament to our friendship that we were able to do that, but for the weaker friendships this can be a really distancing time. I had to start thinking about my career post uni whilst she was settled in a job that she loved, so I definitely felt like I was dragging behind.

Moving into your twenties and stepping onto the career ladder can be a defining moment for a group of friends. Sometimes you move at a different pace and as a result your lives start heading in different directions, which can really challenge a friendship. How do you transition a childhood friend into your adult life if you both operate in different worlds or are moving in entirely different directions? Every friendship group goes through growing pains and it's become even more apparent to me in recent years that my close friendship group all seem to be moving at different paces. For some it's marriage and babies straight away, whilst for others it's all about the career and working their way up the ladder. I have some friends who work up until 9pm just to make sure they're fully prepared for their meetings the next day, whereas others leave at 5pm on the dot because they value their time at home more. There will always be the more academic kids in school but it's not until you enter the *real* world of work that you realise, in terms of drive and ambition, we can all have completely different expectations. As someone who is very career-driven (although not at all academic) I found it confusing and frustrating when friends undervalued themselves and chose what I considered 'the easy option'. I would spend every free day I had interning at PR agencies or working as a runner in advert production, filling my book of contacts for future jobs in the process. I was terrified to not be busy, so I'd work for next to nothing to gain experience and add another line to my CV, but I'd think, why are they not doing this too? I'd quiz a friend over their future plans and stress them out putting pressure on something that maybe wasn't right for them. For me, finding a dream job and getting on the property ladder was incredibly important, but it took a while for me to realise that wasn't a top priority for all of my friends. When you're so sure of something yourself it can be hard to understand why it may be right for you, but not for everyone.

There are some people who travel a lot for work and it can be hard to maintain friendships when you're constantly juggling time zones and fighting with jet lag. Being on a work trip is so all-consuming that when you're out for dinner with clients it's unlikely you're thinking, *It's 8pm at home – maybe I should call my friend.* I find that if I go away for work and I forget to stay in touch with people, I make a point of catching up when I'm back. I'll text when I land, put a date in the diary and use the return from a trip as an excuse to meet up. Even if there are parts of the work trip that you don't really want to discuss, there are always experiences you can share to involve them in what you've been up to. My friends often text me to say, 'Remind me where you have been and where you are going,' and I don't mind if they can't remember, I'm just happy that they care and want to know. As 'the busy one', I can't expect my friends to keep tabs on me, so I'll text them a photo of where I am and say, 'Hi from New York,' to keep us connected.

What if you're the sort of person who has a 40/60 work–life balance but your best friend is 80/20 on a good day? She puts so much of her time and effort into work that it leaves you feeling like she has no time left for you and you have to squeeze in time to see each other like it's just another meeting in her overcrowded iCal. She's not able to switch off so all she does is talk about work and gradually, as you make less of an effort to maintain it, your friendship fades away. I think unless you really understand their work life it's difficult to judge or ask questions, but being there to make sure the '20' is enjoyable and relaxing is how you can be a good friend. I think letting them figure out their work–life balance is all you can really do and it's normal for it to take some time to find a pace that suits you both.

Whilst some friends might enrol in further study or work unpaid to gain experience in a new field, others might attain a huge salary in their very first job. Who can forget the iconic scene in *F.R.I.E.N.D.S* where the group find themselves in different financial places with half of them wanting to go out to the theatre and for dinner and the others feeling embarrassed and awkward that they can't afford it? Money can create a divide amongst even the best of friends; there may be some who are happy to split the bill and others who want to pay £9.46 for their meal because they had tap water and everyone else had wine. Maybe you're lucky and you have a friend who you can talk openly with about money – you can discuss your salary expect-ations and how to negotiate that pay rise – but it's more common for us to avoid the money chat with friends at all costs, *excuse the pun*. We assume how much money our friends make based on their job type, their lifestyle and the investments they make. In modern relationships, getting onto the property ladder can often be a priority over marriage and children and let's not pretend, we all know the first thing we do when a friend buys a property is search for it online to find out the details.

Maybe in some way we use our friends' big decisions to set the pace for our own? There's usually one person in a group of female friends who is always the first; she knows her life plan and the others let her set the pace. As we start 'adulting' it can be an amazing bonding time for friends to share advice and become closer through doing so, but there's no denying it can also leave friends feeling distant if one is moving much faster than the other. After coming out of a ten-year relationship that started in her teens, one of my friends had to essentially start from scratch and start dating again in her mid-twenties. We were all so happy for her when she eventually found someone she really liked as she was always the one with the life plan, you know, the one who we always thought would make a great mum. But obviously meeting someone as an adult is completely different to meeting someone when you're young and they both knew exactly what they wanted and knew immediately that they'd found 'the one'. They moved in together and a year later got engaged, which we were all genuinely over the moon about. At this point, though, I was living with my parents and boyfriend of seven years, so no matter how happy I felt for her, I couldn't not notice that we clearly weren't in the same place. When your friends hit huge milestones in their life, I think it's only human for you to question if you're moving at the right pace yourself. My feelings towards it made me realise that I *was* ready to get engaged and that I wanted it more than I had thought, but our pace was slightly different and that was OK. Now that my friends are starting to get pregnant and have kids, I do worry about us all staying close, but you can't change your own pace for others so I just try to make sure that we accept our different life stages and we don't compare or compete.

Often, those who have moved away from home into a more urban lifestyle can find friends who've opted to stay at home moving faster; they start buying properties, getting married and having babies. It's easy to feel rushed and threatened by the speed they're moving at, and it's important to take a step back to think, *Is that really what I want?* I have friends who have agonised about getting engaged, talking of nothing else for months, only to find that when they do it doesn't satisfy them like they thought it would. It's easy to convince yourself that you want what others have and to be blind to what's right for you.

I remember when I was younger I'd fantasise about getting pregnant at the same time as my best friend. We'd experience it together and recreate scenes from our favourite rom-coms with matching pregnancy dungarees, long buggy walks, and mutual eye rolling at cringeworthy baby classes. We'd shop for baby essentials together and *obviously* our kids would become best friends too! The reality of what happens is obviously quite different. When the time actually comes we can find ourselves in very different places; some feel ready and coo over passing prams whilst others refuse invitations to baby showers and avoid children-friendly BBQs at all costs. I always thought I'd be married with kids by 27 but on my 27th birthday I found myself still living at home saving up to buy my first flat. What if friends start getting pregnant but you're almost at the height of your career, unable (and not wanting) to slow down? What if the choice is taken out of your hands altogether and conceiving a baby proves more difficult than you'd hoped? How do you find the strength to be happy for your friends who get pregnant straight away? You can be happy for someone but at the same time feel heartbroken and inevitably, spending time with friends who just remind you of your struggle is incredibly difficult. I haven't had children yet, although some of my friends have, and when speaking to my older sisters who have five kids between them they say a lot can change in a friendship once you do. It's a huge life change and although at the beginning it's an exciting development within your friendship group, as a mum, it can be easier to surround yourself with other mums.

My sister Jojo felt she didn't have the time or energy to invest in the 'in-between' friends, the ones who weren't old friends but also weren't very recent friends. It was these friendships that required a lot of her attention and ended up fizzling out because as a new mum she struggled with the amount of time she could realistically commit to her friendships. She felt lucky to have so much love around her but at times it was difficult to juggle everything. A friend wants to be there for you and check in on you, but at the same time all of your love and attention is being focused on this new person in your life and maybe they don't quite understand? In fact, my sister said her friends really didn't understand, but she doesn't blame them; until you have a child you don't know what it's really like. She found herself spontaneously speaking to strangers with babies because she naturally felt a connection to those who were also going through what she was. One of her first new 'mum friends' was made in the waiting room of a doctor's surgery, but she also found herself speaking to mums in cafes and at baby groups; she was so drawn to talking to other mums because she found it a great comfort.

From her experience, it's up until around the age of four that you can encourage your kids to be friends and play with the kids of those you want to hang out with, but when they start going to school that's a whole other story and you start having your friendships dictated by your child's. You find yourself friends with women of completely different ages, interests and perspectives and other than your kids being friends, you may not have anything else in common whatsoever. From speaking with my sisters I know that it can be hard to decipher when a mum friend crosses the line over to a *real* friend, and then what if your kids decide they're no longer friends? It seems that unless you all have children at the same time your female friendships can go through a tough time, but I feel reassured after speaking to my sisters that the ones who have been there for a while will continue to be there for you, even if you have to give them less attention for a little while. Fast-forward thirty years or so and maybe, like my mum, some of their best and closest friends will be the other mums they met in those early school years.

But what happens if you're the friend? The one without the new, shiny baby and graphic birth story in tow. How do you steer the fate of your friendship when the changes are totally out of your control? At first, being told by your friend that she's pregnant is actually quite a special moment, especially if you're chosen as one of the first to be told. Just like being a maid of honour, being the best friend during pregnancy gives you a sense of importance; you get nicknamed 'Auntie' and before you know it you're cooing over baby scans, organising a shower and discussing potential names together. Seeing a friend you love do something as incredible as growing a baby can really bring you closer, both sharing the excitement and nerves together. But being pregnant and actually becoming a full-time parent are two different things and it can be a real adjustment when a friend becomes a mum overnight. After giving them space to find their feet in their new role, does it ever just go back to how it was before? The friendship is no longer the priority, and popping over unannounced is no longer an option. *I don't know the baby's nap times, I don't know the difference between the Bugaboo Bee and the Chameleon and don't even get me started on breast pumps . . . what the hell is that thing?!* How does the chat so drastically change from what's new in Zara to who stocks better babygrow packs, Next or Mothercare?

There's a whole new vocabulary that comes with being a mum and if you're not one yourself you can feel completely alienated, nodding along in agreement and then googling frantically on the way home. As the non-parent friend, it's a struggle to find the balance between being understanding of this new chapter in your friend's life and not excluding them from their 'old' life. It's all about balance – there's nothing wrong with going on a big night out with other friends, BUT follow it up with a night in and takeaway or a walk during the day that everyone can join in on. This is still quite a new stage for my friends and me but so far, I've found that the love I have for my friends has completely translated itself onto their kids. So, I've only felt positive things towards what I like to think of as 'growing our friendship group'. In fact, when our friend got pregnant, we changed the name of the WhatsApp group to '+1 Mini W', welcoming him into our group before he was even born. It's likely that there will be times when my mum friends can't be as spontaneous as they once were and I might have to call upon other friends for the attention they can't give me, but after speaking to my sister and hearing how hard it was for her to be a new mum and maintain her friendships, I know it's up to me to put in extra effort whilst they figure out their new roles as mums.

My sister Carly has a lot of different friends, but amongst them are two whom she's been close with since she was really young. For me, her group of three friends is the ultimate example of how best friends can stay close despite all of them taking completely different paths in life. They met at school when they were seven, but didn't really start socialising together until secondary school. They were part of a bigger group, but the bond between them as a threesome became stronger and stronger as they started to social-ise outside of school and eventually started going on summer holidays. They experienced all of their firsts together, which is what my sister says really bonded them so tight. They didn't always stick together though: one left school to attend a different sixth form, they went to different places in their gap year and then when it came to university they were scattered all over the UK. They'd speak regularly during uni, always messaging and calling, but they only visited each other once, so the friendship never relied so much on seeing each other.

The thing with their friendship is that the bond created early on was so strong that they always had confidence that any new friends they made would never replace what they had with each other. The role they play in each other's lives is like an unspoken loyalty with a deep understanding of how each other feels about situations – without having to explain it. They were always each other's rocks and they'd have each other's backs, it was never a doubt in their mind. As they grew into their adult lives they all took different directions; one chose further study, working on a PhD, another chose to have kids pretty soon and moved abroad to build a large family, the other (my sister) started her own business and then went on to have kids, juggling both. Now, in their late thirties they all live in different places, some abroad, all moving at a different pace with completely different priorities, but it has never affected their closeness. They all have their own 'other' friends but there's an unsaid under-standing that wherever they are in the world, nothing changes.

It's not about how often they see each other or speak, it's gone past the point where that would even matter. Their friendship is like a safety net and my sister says often what happens is she'll be thinking about her friend (who lives abroad) and then she'll get a text message from her saying hi. They know more about each other than their sisters do because they know the stuff that siblings wouldn't need to know unless it was specifically relevant. They've learnt from years of leading separate lives that it's just so impor-tant to keep in touch; they'll always message each other first with any news or updates or give up time to talk for hours on the phone if one is struggling with a situation. I asked if they ever argued; she said they know each other well enough that they know how to approach any confrontation and more specifically *when* to approach it, so it doesn't upset them and end up as an argument. No matter where they've ended up, the friendships have remained just as important as they always were. It's not easy to keep hold of all your friends and keep the closeness that's so special, espe-cially when distance comes between you.

LONG-DISTANCE
FRIENDSHIPS

At 18 we all got the buzz of freedom as we finished school. Some chose to start their careers, some went straight into higher education but I got the travel bug and worked for a few months to save up for a round-the-world plane ticket. There were a few of my friends who chose to travel together and we were happy to group off and give each other space, knowing it wasn't permanent. We then spent our early twenties figuring shit out and we were spread all around the UK. But because we're all Londoners and our families live there, we naturally all kept coming back. It was in my late twenties that I noticed a divide amongst my friends: those who wanted to move abroad and those who wanted to stay put. I grew up in the capital and I've always loved the city and never had any plans to move away. I can only imagine my kids having the same upbringing that I had and being close to my family is incredibly important to me. This means I naïvely assumed my friends would feel the same way and honestly, I felt quite shocked when I started hearing of their ideas to try living out of the UK.

Whatever the reason is to move, whether it's a compromise for their partner, work, or simply because they want to, as a friend it's hard to embrace that huge life decision that affects you both. I've always been proud of the type of friend I am and I know that I have the ability to put myself second and prioritise a friend's happiness, but the only time I struggle to hide my self-ish emotions seems to be when they choose to move abroad. When I feel strongly about something I often find it hard to understand an opposing point of view, it's one of my worst qualities, and being close to family is something I feel passionate about. It's why I never win the argument with Anna when I try to convince her to move back to London, because we both know living near family is the best and I can't argue with that! I also think, equal to my family, what would always stop me from moving away are my friends. Sure, we could speak regularly and I'm sure we'd stay close despite the distance but I don't *want* to; I love seeing my friends and I would never want to move away from them, I don't understand when others do.

When my friend Keisha, who I've known for 26 years, decided to try out her modelling career in New York, I felt full of pride and excitement for her. Being a full-time working model was all I ever wanted for her; it took her a long time to gain the confidence to put herself out there so as her friend I totally encouraged it. At first it was a lot of travelling back and forth so it didn't feel permanent and catching up over FaceTime was really exciting; we actually had so much more to discuss and living through her adventures was a positive and motivating thing for me. Over time, New York became more of a permanent home for her and asking, 'When are you next home?' started to feel like a bit of an empty question. She'd book outbound flights with no return and as someone who likes to plan, I hated the uncertainty and the words 'no return' just made my heart sink. The place that was a holiday destination to me became more of a home to her and when I was able to go over to visit I could see how settled she really was.

Selfishly, in those first couple of years, I found comfort in her homesickness; knowing she was longing to be back home gave me hope for her return and as she settled in I felt conflicted between my happiness for her and my own sadness. I guess part of my fear is due to the fact that I know, as a friend, I'm better face to face. I was never the teenager who spent hours on the phone to friends in the evenings; I'm terrible at phone calls, I've always found them to be so awkward. Maybe it's because I like to bounce off someone's facial expressions or body language but the fear I have for a prolonged silence on a phone call is real. I used to panic and find ways to cut the conversation short, like faking my mum calling me for dinner, just to avoid any awkwardness. But texts can be equally hard to nail; I worry that the tone of voice in my texts may come across wrongly and then I become paranoid that I've been misunderstood. If I don't get a reply for a while I worry they've been in some dramatic deadly accident . . . trust me, I'm just better face to face.

Keisha was my first friend to move away and even five years later I'm still not sure I've got the knack for long-distance communication. We're lucky that because of the length of our friendship there's no real threat of drifting apart. As 'the childhood friend' she'll always know and love me, and our memories are so rich that there's no risk of awkwardness or a lack of connection; when we see each other it's like it's been no time at all. The struggle is in keeping the friendship current and not relying on reminiscing about the past, but working on pushing the friendship forward and making new memories together. I find with long-distance friendships that you spend most of the time catching up on work, family and daily life but with friends you see and speak to regularly those things are already known so you can skip 'How are you?' and get straight into deeper chat. Sometimes the real moments in life happen completely unexpectedly and so it's difficult to experience new memories together when phone calls are scheduled and chatting time is forced. I'm lucky that over the years our overlapping work trips have meant I've been able to visit her a few times but last year Keisha moved to Jamaica . . . *don't even get me started on that.* JAMAICA! Are you kidding me?! As her life moves in a different direction and she settles down where she wants, we're continuing to learn how to maintain our friendship and we both know it's totally worth the hard work. Over the years we've both developed some tips for keeping in touch that have really helped.

TIPS FOR KEEPING LDFs ACTIVE

- If time zones are an issue, using voice notes on WhatsApp adds a real personal touch to your quick messages. It's so nice to hear a familiar voice and is a great alternative to texting.
- Add your friend's location into the World Clock on your smart phone so you can always be aware of what time is it for her.
- Be spontaneous; FaceTime calls don't have to be at night when you're at home, if you're out and see something you think they'd like to see, give them a call. Not every call has to be a long one.
- Be thoughtful. Send birthday cards and presents, send flowers for special occasions, but you also don't need a reason to send a funny card that reminded you of them.
- If you can, make a plan to go and visit, but if you can't, just show an interest – ask to see photos of where they're living or a video tour!

With one friend living in Jamaica, another considering a move to Australia and the other insisting her boyfriend won't settle down until they try living abroad for a while, I do feel nervous about where my female friendships will be in ten years' time. But I think it's important to be flexible and deal with the situations that life throws at you because if a friendship is worth it you should work hard to maintain it. I have to accept there may be changes in how my friendships work and they might not always be how I envisaged them.

... *the one who serves a purpose*

THE ONCE-IN-A-BLUE-MOON FRIEND

The OIBMF (catchy eh?) never quite makes it into the best friend zone. You meet up with them a few times a year and, don't get me wrong, it's always great, but it is what it is and it requires minimal effort. The OIBMF serves a purpose – maybe their intense drive gives you the motivational boost you need or their calming nature lends itself well when you're feeling stressed. Your lives don't sync so the friendship never moves forward but the time you spend together is always memorable and *it just works.*

———

Do: *Enjoy the time you spend with them and live in the moment.*

Don't: *Add pressure to make the friendship more complicated; accept it for what it is.*

184

THE FRIEND
MATCHMAKER

Something I've always found really helpful when maintaining my friendships is merging and introducing friends. It's rare for me to have a friend who hasn't met the rest, but it wasn't until researching for this book and speaking to others that I realised this isn't that common. A lot of people like to keep their friends separate and don't expect them to get on with each other. I think for me, when I make a new friend, part of me wants to share my shiny new toy and show it off to my other friends, and if I meet someone who I think is great my natural instinct is to tell my friends all about them. I also find it's really helpful when making a new friend to introduce them to the people who know me best so they can really understand me and what kind of friend I am to others. I can only be 100% myself around my best friends and only they know the *real* me. I do try and think about personalities and who will get on with who, because realistically you can't expect everyone to bond, but I've introduced a lot of friends who have gone on to develop friendships that exist independently without me as the glue.

I genuinely think friend matchmaking is one of my life skills. Most of my friends are very easy-going and will make an effort to get on with anyone, but I'm usually really excited to introduce people when I think they share some common ground. I have a mental tick list that I work from; I think about their interests, their current life situation and their personality traits. For example, I wouldn't make the effort to introduce a very argumentative friend to another strongly opinionated friend because all that's going to do is cause uncomfortable confrontation during dinner *but* I would introduce someone very funny to a friend who embraces banter well without getting offended. I do it in small batches, taking two couples out at a time, and I'm good at getting conversations going. I give them something to talk about, pointing out their similarities or loose connections, and then I sit back and watch the magic happen.

It is a strange feeling though when two friends who

LILY PEBBLES

you introduced start to see each other without you and maybe at first, I feel a bit left out (I mean, I *was* the one who told them about the brunch place so . . .), but in the long term it really is such a positive thing. When you know there's always an open invitation it's actually a really warm and fuzzy feeling knowing the people you love enjoy each other's company too. Keeping up with friends is a lot of work so, if anything, being able to meet up with a few at a time is an enjoyable convenience and it makes birthdays and other social occasions easier too!

187

WE WERE ON
A BREAK

We hear about the huge friendship fallouts and cute friendship make-ups, but what about the friendship break? What about the friendships that fizzle out for no reason at all and then years later, fall back into place and pick up where they left off?

One of my oldest friends who I've known since I was five sent me a quote from Instagram that read, *'Shout out to the friendships that are strong enough to withstand busy spells, mood swings, and weird distant phases. True friendship is rare, man.'* And it couldn't be truer for us. We drifted apart through our university years, having one of those 'weird distant phases', always still caring for one another but there was a serious lack of communication. We were leading different lives, making new friends, and although we were the oldest of friends, for a time we weren't the closest. I wasn't part of the group who planned her hen party, nor was I involved much in the wedding at all, but it's what felt right for us at the time and I didn't take offence – I knew she had other friends she was closer with. That was three years ago and it's crazy how much can change because now we are closer than we've ever been and those distant years are something we really laugh about. After we finished university and settled back in London, we were both in serious relationships and found ourselves with more in common than we'd had throughout the past few years. The initial bond we'd had years ago meant we could just pick up where we left off, but it was even stronger than before.

I think it's OK to have breaks in a friendship; in fact I think it can be healthy. A friend of mine had a similar situation; she grew up with a group of four friends who were inseparable through secondary school. As they went their separate ways for university they found that one went off on a different path, hanging out with a very different crowd of people, getting herself into situations that the others didn't feel comfortable with. It meant that for those few years, although they didn't phase her out on purpose, they just naturally grew apart. They stayed friends online, seeing what the other was up to, but never really engaged in conversation. Eventually they bumped into each other years later and one made the first move to say hi, purely because she genuinely missed her. They started hanging out again and the break was never really discussed; she was in a better place with new friends and a new boyfriend and they all just knew that the break had been a temporary thing and they entered the next phase of their friendship. When I asked why she didn't feel hurt from the years of lack of communication she said it was down to the fact that the group of four wasn't all they had. They had friend-ships that existed outside of that four, which really took the pressure off and meant they could take the space they all needed without feeling alone.

Some friendship breaks are inevitable and they naturally arise as a way of giving the relationship space for you to grow individually, but can a break ever be enforced and have a positive outcome? Honestly, I don't know the answer. The question is, what is the best way to deal with a break? Do you let it happen naturally or confront the issue? When you find yourself growing apart from someone, you hope that they feel the same way too, you can both make less effort and before you know it you haven't spoken for months and it's fine – technically, it's both your faults. But what if it's just one of you that feels like you need a break? If a friend said they needed space, would you be offended? I say, put yourself in their position and do what you would want them to do to you; maybe that means sitting down for an honest and kind chat or maybe it means making less of an effort to communicate and letting the friendship just fade out.

THE BFFN

When I look back at the different stages of my adult life so far, whether I was volunteering at London Fashion Week, working my way up the career ladder in beauty or networking my way around the blogosphere, there was usually a BFFN (Best Friend For Now) close by. You know the ones, the friends who without any warning just appear in your life at the most perfect time and sweep you off your feet. The planets align, your paths cross and at that time she is just what you need in a friend and so naturally she becomes your everything. Before you know it you're inseparable, she shoots up the rankings as a potential new BFF and the memories you make together are golden. You spend all of your time together, it's so exciting, it's fresh . . . it's that new friend romance we all love so much. But it's not until years later that you realise in fact they were not a real BFF, but only a BFFN, and not only did it not last but you didn't even notice it fizzle out. The BFFN is the one you speak of in the past tense: 'Do you remember that girl I was really close with a couple of years ago?' At the time you were great for each other but your lives went in different directions and neither party fought for the friendship. Maybe you helped each other get to the next life milestone or you gave each other a confidence boost during a time when you really needed it. What's memorable about the BFFN is that the experiences you had together and the lessons you learned from that relationship continue to live on, even if the friendship didn't.

My friend has experienced this with someone she became close with during her maternity leave. They found each other at the right time, when their lives were in sync. Having a newborn baby and suddenly being off work every day meant that she had to be open to making new types of friends. But although they became incredibly close for those first couple of years, she found that as she'd gradually got back into her career, their pre-baby life was actually quite different and they didn't have as much in common as they thought. For that short period of her life, that friend was perfect and everything she needed, but not every friend is forever; some are just good for that moment in time.

After university, I spent a year interning at different PR agencies, trying to figure out what I liked and disliked and where I wanted to try and find a job. I made friends with a fellow intern and we really hit it off; we spent every lunchtime together and instead of competing we took the opportunity to push and support each other through a time when we felt a bit lost, unsure of where our careers were headed and what our future held. It was whilst working there that I received my university results via email and I'll never forget that day and how it felt. It was really emotional but completely strange as I had no real friends or family around me, just unfamiliar colleagues and my one new friend. Sharing the news with her and her being there to witness my immediate reaction and emotions brought us closer together and after that she chose to confide in me about her future, which is now something I look back on as her defining BFFN moment.

She was midway through university, studying fashion, but during her break she was faced with a massive life decision and chose to ask me for advice. She'd been offered her dream job doing the PR for one of her all-time favourite fashion labels but dropping out of university was a huge decision and something she wasn't sure of. We spent our lunchtimes going back and forth, discussing the pros and the cons, how she saw her future panning out and fundamentally establishing her gut feelings towards the decision. I was there as a sounding board, a neutral opinion away from family and friends, but with industry knowledge and a personal opinion that she respected. She went on to inform her university that she was leaving and accepted her dream job; before I knew it she was off and our personal and career paths took entirely different directions. Aside from the odd Facebook 'like' here and there we barely stayed in touch but I have since stalked her on LinkedIn and found out that she kept that dream job for quite a few years.

Although we are no longer friends it's nice to know that I was a part of her journey somehow and that maybe she also looks back on me as her BFFN. We came together and although she made less of an impact on me than I did on her, seeing her make such a bold decision definitely inspired me when it came to taking up potential job opportunities. The friendship wasn't left sour and it wasn't explosive in any way, it was perfect as it was and it happened for a reason. I'm not a very spiritual person but I do believe people come into our lives at certain times for a set purpose. Naturally your life has different chapters and you learn different things about yourself in each one thanks to the characters who weave in and out. The BFFN is a more concentrated friendship than most, a friendship fling if you will. It's intense and it's short but it can be really powerful and leave you with long-lasting memories.

Maybe not all of my experiences have been positive but they all seemed to serve a purpose; even if I look back and cringe at how I thought someone might become best-friend material, reflecting on why it didn't work out really helps me with making future friends. In the past, I have experienced an intense friendship that left me feeling a bit used. I met a girl who I thought I could be really close friends with; we went from zero to 100 in a couple of weeks, suddenly spending all our time together and messaging daily. She met my friends and my family and I met hers. Once I decide I trust someone, I completely open up and let them in, introducing them to the important people in my life and being there to support them in whatever way they need. I noticed as the friendship progressed that she always asked me *a lot* of questions, one after the other in a really persistent way, often about work, life organisation or how I felt about certain topics. In the beginning of a friendship you often need time to warm up so at first I didn't notice, but as the friendship progressed I realised we would never just have casual conversations, it was as if she only gave me her time when she needed something from me.

A couple of years after meeting her, she'd made another new close friend and it really made me see our friendship in its true light, as I saw her befriend this girl in the same way she did to me. She showered her with attention, invited her into her life, made her feel special and then started with the intense questioning. She wasn't looking for true friends, she was looking for the best in people and then trying so intensely to take it from them, learning any skills or knowledge they had for herself. It wasn't ever clear whether she truly wanted to be friends or if she was using me, and the uncertainty made me feel uncomfortable, so naturally I distanced myself from her, being more wary of what to share. It was a shame, but really it was more a shame for her because a life without real, honest friendships must be a very lonely, boring one. It made me think more about my adult friendships and the importance of taking more time to get to know someone before giving them my all. When a two-year friendship ends and you both feel like you gained something from it then it can be looked back on as a special relationship, but sometimes you can look back and think, *I helped them with their career, social life and self-confidence, but what exactly did I get out of it?* There's always something you can take away from a friendship experience, especially the negative ones. I can now look back on friendships like this and learn from them, reading the signs if I think someone is just using me to get something or get to someone.

> **@tflquotes 11th October 2017 Farringdon Station**
>
> The Lesson:
> - Not everyone you love will stay.
> - Not everyone you trust will be loyal.
> - Some people only exist as examples of what to avoid.

But not all BFFNs are bad experiences; I think in most cases they're looked back on with fond memories. A friend of mine met someone during a work event, giving a talk to kids struggling at school, and they clicked straight away feeling inspired by each other's stories. From that day on they were inseparable; they spoke every day and saw each other at least once or twice a week and this lasted for around two years.

When they met initially the friendship was based on a 'big sister–little sister' relationship but as the years went on, my friend (who was always the little sister of the two) felt she'd really grown into herself and become more confident in her decisions. She no longer felt like the 'little sister' character who let the other one always be in charge; she felt more assertive and was less concerned with pleasing her 'big sister' friend. But they hadn't grown at the same time and her friend wasn't willing to give up her role or accept the changes and growth that the other had made. They never confronted the change or argued about it, but the friendship gradually fizzled out as they realised they didn't fit together anymore. It's been two years since they spoke and this year, my friend held out an olive branch, inviting her old friend to her birthday drinks. She didn't even have her current mobile number but she dug out her email address and sent off an invite not knowing if she'd get a reply. She replied immediately saying she'd be there and she was; since then they've been speaking almost daily again. Maybe now time has passed, they can try picking up where they left off. When I asked her what had changed, she said she felt as if her friend had grown, she was more trusting now, more confident and expected less of her. They've found themselves back in the right place, at the right time, but clearly someone always has to make the first move . . .

#AskLP

Growing up my mom always told me not to trust my friends as she'd had so many people backstab her or put her in bad situations. So, I don't have many friends but I'm super close to my sisters but I do wish I had more close friends.

I think it's really nice that you're close with your sisters. Don't write them off as friends; the friendships you have with them can be just as, if not more, special than ones you have with other female friends. But if you genuinely do wish you had more close friends then I think it's a shame your mum doesn't let you learn from your own experiences. She was obviously really let down and heartbroken by her friends and therefore wants to protect you, but I think in life you need to learn from your own mistakes as they'll probably lead you onto something great. Try not to let your mum's bad experiences stop you making new friends and be brave enough to discover for yourself who to become close with, and if it makes you feel better, do so with your sisters!

TOXIC FRIENDSHIPS

Toxic friendships: we hear about them all the time, whether it's an article on ten ways to quit them or a newsletter encouraging you to 'Tackle your toxic friendships this month'. It seems we all have them, but why do we allow them to continue? Why all the tips on how to manage them in the media? I think this is because most of us still don't really know if we're in a toxic friendship or not. So, let's rewind for a second. Before we try to cure what is, without a doubt, the most negative type of female friendship, let's figure out how we know when we're in one!

WHAT IS A TOXIC FRIENDSHIP?

A toxic friendship isn't defined by a one-off negative experience, but instead an on-going negativity that taints the friendship at every opportunity. It can be one-sided or toxic from multiple angles; either way, someone is suffering and it is affecting them in an unhelpful and sometimes damaging way.

HOW TO IDENTIFY A TOXIC FRIENDSHIP

In a dream world, our potential new friends would all be walking around with signs on their heads like 'listener', 'gossiper', 'advice giver', 'flaky', so that we'd know at first glance exactly what we're letting ourselves in for. But unfortunately (or probably fortunately for some of us), they don't and so identifying whether a friendship is toxic or not comes down to realising how that friend makes you feel. How do you feel after spending time with them? Do they affect how you behave as a person? Is the friendship equal?

It's not always obvious but only you know whether a friendship makes a positive impact on your life or whether it subtracts more than it adds. Maybe you feel down after spending time together, or you're drained of all emotions? When everyone around you seems to love spending time with their BFF, do you dread spending time with yours? Sometimes you can be completely blind to it until it's pointed out by someone close to you, like a parent or a sibling, who can see how it's affecting your behaviour. There are so many ways in which a friendship can be toxic, which is why I think it's still so common and hard to identify.

THE TOXIC TYPES

The Green Monster

Jealousy in any relationship is toxic; it's probably the most common emotion to destroy friendships, but it can often go undetected until it finally attacks. The thing is, there is a huge difference between envy and jealousy, and that's really where the fine line is within a friendship. Envy is a normal human emotion and being envious of a friend can be flattering in a way, if it's dealt with properly. Saying to a friend, 'Oh my God, I'm so jealous you got that bag, it's gorgeous,' isn't *real* jealousy and airing it out loud is actually a great way of diminishing any truly jealous feelings. It's the darker, real jealousy that's a killer, the quiet one that we don't talk about so much. The type of jealousy that takes any positivity and turns it into something nega-tive. Every positive experience gives the opportunity for a friend to be jealous; maybe it's your lifestyle or career opportunities, or that you're spending time with other friends. Maybe you fell in love or you're starting a family; you see, the older we get and the more these milestones mean to us, the more opportunity there is for jealousy. But the older we get, the easier it becomes to air our envy and prevent any true jealousy brewing. Jealousy within a friendship is toxic because fundamentally, jealousy prioritises your own emotions, wants and needs over a friend's. There's no comforting a jealous friend; they want what you have and therefore they can't feel happy about what you've achieved. You might exert so much energy on downplaying your achievements but eventually the guilt will turn into anger and you'll realise that a real friend should be happy and supportive no matter what.

Real friends celebrate each other's successes and feel secure enough in their own accomplishments that they don't feel the need to 'one-up' each other. Have you ever told a friend some good news only to be cut off by their more important news? I have. It starts to feel like a game of achievement tennis: 'I got a promotion at work', 'OMG so funny, so did I *and* they've given me a pay rise!' A jealous friend will regularly use the word 'unfair', making your gain their loss. Instead of building you up they'll try to drag you down to their level at every opportunity, with a competitive streak that's ready to take over and leave you behind at any point. Jealousy breeds all kinds of unhealthy competition and it's painfully toxic.

> *Tip: Calm the Green Monster by sharing a time when you may have felt jealous of them and remind them how you handled it well and didn't compete.*

The Jellyfisher

In 2004, the wonderful human that is Bridget Jones not only made us feel less alone in our painful First-World problems, but she introduced us to the friend we've all experienced but have never quite been able to label correctly . . .

The Jellyfisher – a person who always inserts a veiled, stinging remark into a general conversation.

Things a Jellyfisher would say . . .

'Do you remember that nice dress you wore to my birthday last year when you were thinner?'

'Your new boyfriend is gorgeous; how did you manage that?'

'Well done on your new job, I didn't think you were qualified for that!'

Sting. Sting. Sting.

It can take a while to identify these types of friends because they can be quite manipulative and because backhanded compliments are really quite peculiar things. They leave you feeling confused, trying to understand how something that sounded quite like a compliment has left you feeling sad inside. The Jellyfisher deflects their unhappiness and their insecurities onto you, using it as a way to bring you down so that they can feel bigger and better about themselves. A friend who puts you down will often disguise their insult as 'just being honest' or 'trying to be helpful', putting the blame on you for taking it the wrong way. It's all a bit of a mindfuck . . .

> *Tip: This is their bad quality not yours, so learn how to be prepared for it and not let it upset you. Reply with a confident answer that will completely throw them.*

The Energy Vampire

Have you ever asked a friend a question and then half an hour later noticed they're still talking about themselves and seem to have no plans to stop and ask you a question back? Friendship is a balancing act and the exchange needs to be somewhat equal. The question is, are they there for you as much as you are there for them? We all have different personalities so I don't think you can expect your friends to behave in the exact same way as you do; maybe you're more of an open book and they like to be more private. But how do you know if your friendship is an equal one? Visualise it on a set of weighing scales . . . every time a friend leans on you for support, tells you a story about themselves or asks you for advice, your side of the scales dips, and the same vice versa. So how does your friendship weigh up? The sort of friend who takes more than they give is emotionally draining and therefore damaging to your own ability to care for yourself. If every time you confide in her for help she turns it into an opportunity to talk about herself, your problems are pushed to the side and left unmanaged. The Energy Vampire is the friend who takes and takes, who constantly leaves you feeling drained and negative and surrounds you with a vibe that is unhealthy and unwanted. We all have friends who require a bit more time and love but the Energy Vampire takes it that little bit further, to where it begins to feel more like a free therapy session than a friendship.

As the 'older sister friend' my mum has found herself in quite a few toxic friendships in the past. Having friendships that last for over 40 years means that over time things are bound to change and a friendship can turn into something completely different from how it started.

She was in her twenties when she met Sally, who was the life and soul of the party; she had the most bubbly, contagious and upbeat personality. Everybody loved her, in fact my mum felt she was almost in her shadow, but Sally took her under her wing, helped her get her dream job in London and their friendship grew stronger and stronger. As time went on they continued to be friends, seeing each other slightly less as their lives took different paths but always meeting up monthly and catching up on the phone. When Sally's marriage ended it was tough for my mum to see a friend who was usually so full of life falling apart at the seams. She was there for her through the tough times but things never really felt the same as her outlook on life had so drastically changed. She noticed over time that the scales had shifted and the friendship had become far more one-sided than it had been before. Giving her the benefit of the doubt and remembering the good times, my mum would accept a coffee meet-up only to leave wondering why she had thought it would be better than the last. Sally began to rely on her more and more, only ever speaking about herself and her problems, never asking or listening to anything in return. Eventually she felt she had to set some boundaries; she stopped meeting Sally for coffee and instead spoke just on the phone.

Years passed, not much changed; Sally still only ever spoke about herself and it became so intense it would leave my mum feeling completely mentally drained. I remember this phase from my teenage years; she'd phone our house at 6pm, 'Muuuuum, Sally's on the phone!' She'd prop the phone up between her ear and shoulder, sometimes even throughout dinner whilst listening for over an hour, rarely ever getting the chance to speak. This went on for years. Knowing Sally was obviously going through a hard time my mum never had the courage to cut ties until one day she went too far. It was when my grandma passed away; Sally phoned and asked why she hadn't had a call for a while. When hearing the news, instead of showing signs of comfort, sadness or any caring qualities a friend should during this time, she made it about her. 'Why didn't you tell me? I'm so offended you didn't call when it happened!' It took an ugly response like this to show my mum that this wasn't the person she once knew; for whatever reason Sally had become someone else and there was no more my mum could do to help her. All she could do was ignore her phone calls and with all of our encouragement, she chose to prioritise herself for once and cut ties with her Energy Vampire friend.

> *Tip:* Do your best to find the root of the problem, but let it be their choice whether they want to speak to you about it. Confronting someone when they're in a dark place might not be the best thing to do, but reaching out and letting them know you're always there for them could encourage them. Eventually you have to prioritise yourself; give the friendship some space so you can revisit it one day, knowing you did all that you could at the time.

The Glory Hunter

It is hugely important within friendships to celebrate each other's successes, to acknowledge when a friend deserves a pat on the back, a round of drinks or simply a congratulatory text, but beware of the Glory Hunters. There are some 'friends' who are only there for the good times and only come out of the woodwork when you've achieved something. They only want to be associated with you once you've done something they deem as successful and something worth showing off about. These friends will love to spend time with you when you're in a good mood and when you're being your most fun self, but realistically will they be there for you when you are going through a tough time? *Unlikely.* Not only will this put pressure on you to feel like you always have to be positive in front of them or always have an exciting update to share, but it'll also mean your true feelings and problems – no matter how big or small – will stay locked up inside of you. And that's not a healthy thing to do in any relationship.

> *Tip: Test the friendship and give them a chance to prove you wrong by confiding in them during a time of need or asking for some important advice. If they really are a Glory Hunter this negativity will probably put them off the friendship so you won't have to confront the problem.*

212

The Queen Bee

Hands up who's experienced being friends with a Queen Bee? Most commonly found in our teenage days, the Queen Bee is the ruler of a friendship group, the controller, the manipulator. If *Mean Girls* taught us anything, it's not just that we wear pink on Wednesdays but that no matter how hard we try, it's *very* hard not to be drawn in by the lure of a Regina George. The Queen Bee has Jellyfisher qualities as she has the ability to turn a compliment into the most cutting insult, but what the Queen Bee really has, and what she's really defined by, is power. Queen Bees wield power over their minions; they have you craving any kind of attention or compliment no matter how harsh the insult is to follow. They thrive on intimidation and feed off insecurities but on the outside, they seem kind and caring, pulling you into their web. The Queen Bee is both respected and feared: 'The weird thing about hanging out with Regina was that I could hate her, and at the same time, I still wanted her to like me.'

It all seems pretty petty, right? But the Regina Georges of the world aren't always left behind in our school years. 'The Plastics' live on in adult life and without even realising it you can find yourself feeling trapped in a toxic friendship trying so badly to impress a friend who has some kind of invisible power over you. The Queen Bee is a combination of all the most toxic types of friendship rolled into one seemingly confident powerhouse. I say 'seemingly' because it's likely that under all that noise and confidence there is probably quite an insecure girl who doesn't know how to deal with her emotions. Get close enough and you might see more of her true self, giving you the power to bring out her softer side, and maybe her confidence can somehow inspire you to be more assertive in certain situations.

> **Tip:** *Try to focus your time on another friend for a while, allowing yourself to be out of the bubble and less concerned about what the Queen Bee thinks. You can't control them but you can control yourself, so make some bold decisions, do something for yourself, and prove to them and to yourself that you're not really under their spell.*

HOW TO END A TOXIC FRIENDSHIP

Address the issue as it happens. Maybe you've got into the habit of biting your tongue every time they put you down or you constantly build them up when they express jealousy towards you. See what happens if you gradually start addressing the issues as they arise. Speak up when they do something to upset you and tell them how you feel about what just happened. It's very likely that they don't even realise that they're doing it so by making them aware they might start thinking before they speak.

Take the pressure off them to improve and turn it on yourself. If you're a believer of 'you can't change others so change yourself', look into your own personality, figure out why you've allowed such a relationship to exist and continue to work on improving yourself for future relationships. You're not to blame for a toxic friendship but maybe there is something you can do to make sure you don't get into this situation again. Use the opportunity to become more self-aware and to focus on self-improvement.

Set some boundaries. Maybe you're not quite ready to end your toxic friendship or you know it'll turn into an explosive argument that will only end badly for you. In this case, set some healthy boundaries that you can use to keep the friendship going in a way that is manageable. Learning to say no is a life skill we all need to adopt within all different aspects of our lives. We're constantly told by the media to say yes, to be open to new opportunities, to be adventurous and daring, but when it comes

to mental health and to well-being, more of us are looking into how to say no. This also applies to friendship,
learning it's OK to say no, to politely decline. You don't
have to accept an invitation if you don't want to; try
taking control and organise time with that friend on
your terms. Toxic friendships can be emotionally draining; setting boundaries when it comes to catch-ups can
be a step in the right direction, letting them know they
can't have access to you whenever they want. Something
as simple as 'I'll call you on the way into work' and
setting a time to catch up gives a time limit to the
conversation. Meeting up regularly at set times means
that if they call you out of hours you have the ability to
say, 'I'm just in the middle of something but looking
forward to catching up on Friday!'

Let it go. If the toxicity is at an all-time high and
you've lost all hope for regaining any kind of valuable
friendship then maybe it's just time to let go. Not
everyone is open to change and your happiness trumps
everything else so don't let this one toxic friendship
ruin everything else you have. Let the friendship drift
off, let it turn into a social media relationship, have the
strength to be the flaky friend that you never wanted
to be. You may feel rubbish at first but in the long run
it's probably best for the both of you.

TOXIC TOPICS

Even if you're lucky enough to have avoided toxic friendships, it's quite likely that you will have at least encountered a few toxic topics within your friendship group. A toxic topic can appear from nowhere, completely unexpectedly, and leaves friends in a bewildered 'What just happened?' state. They'll be different for everyone, whether it's politics, religion, current affairs or other – a toxic topic is a controversial topic that has the ability to divide opinions and is something that usually wouldn't come up in discussion until deep into a friendship. It's quite likely that you already vaguely know a friend's opinions on certain topics and whether or not you agree, it's something you're able to respect and agree to disagree on. But toxic topics bring out the worst in friends and it's something I know a lot of people experienced during the 2016 UK general election. It's the fine line between discussing the difference in political parties and what that means for the country, and pushing your opinions onto others and attacking any opposing views. From my personal experience, it's not always *what* is said but *how* it's said. Before you know it, you're discussing really complicated issues that would never usually grace the dinner table and you're left feeling broken by the whole experience. That's when it becomes a toxic topic, something never to be brought up again. It's a risk factor, a threat to your friendship, and it's better left away from the dinner table. Social media and the ability to type your thoughts from behind a screen have further complicated the threat of a toxic topic. We've all had the experience of logging in, reading a status from someone you're 'friends' with and thinking, *How can they possibly have such warped views on life? If this is how they really think, we have nothing in common anymore.* The digital age has only added to the conflict, turning an awkward dinner chat that you can quickly move on from into something more permanent that others can join in on.

According to a recent study, 28% of us hit the 'unfriend' button in 2016 because someone said or shared something political we took offence at. I have a few toxic topics lurking amongst my friendships group, one of which is 'living in London'. My friend's husband has a very strong dislike of living in London and the busy pace of life. He hopes to bring up his kids elsewhere so they can have a less urban upbringing like he did. I was brought up in London, I have lived here my whole life and absolutely love it, flaws and all . . . So, when it came up in conversation over dinner and he listed off the reasons he can't wait to move away, I took offence and started listing off all the reasons why he should feel lucky to live in London. It got very heated, to say the least; you know when your adrenaline kicks in and you feel a bit shaky but you're also desperately trying to keep your cool? Yeh, that's why it became our toxic topic and we haven't brought it up since. Within another group of friends, our toxic topic *believe it or not* is 'Millennial Pink'. I'm really not sure how a group WhatsApp conversation about 'millennials' turned into a debate about whether we subconsciously buy into fashion trends or not, but again, things got heated and awkward very quickly. *Ding ding ding – toxic topic.* Pushed aside, never to be brought up again.

I don't think a toxic topic should be grounds for 'friendivorce'; it's not a sign of a toxic friendship, it's just something that becomes part of that friendship and an equal understanding of where the conversation boundaries lie. I think they're pushed aside and silenced as a way to protect the friendship because no one wants to argue or have friction unnecessarily about something that can be quite unimportant. Through trial and error, as we navigate our way through our adult female friendships, we learn which friends we can discuss certain topics with and which ones to avoid discussing them with at all costs.

... *the one who says it how it is*

THE REALIST FRIEND

The realist friend is the honest, slightly pessimistic and blunt friend all rolled into one. They'll often get labelled as the negative one but it's just because a realist looks at something for what it really is. Pointless or fake positivity is not their thing so don't expect rainbows and ponies. If you ask them *honestly* what they think of your outfit, they'll tell you what they actually think. They're not afraid to speak the truth and it's their best trait at times . . . but also their worst. Need someone to mediate an argument? She's your girl. The realist friend is super laid back . . . if everything goes to plan. Don't be fooled by their happy-go-lucky attitude, it's all been thought through and planned. It wouldn't be wise to find yourself in conflict with the realist friend; she's the one who *loves* an 'I told you so!' She has an answer for everything and the incessant questioning will drive you insane at times, but with the realist friend you know what you're getting and she's always there to listen and give you solid advice.

———

Do: *Feel confident enough to push your positivity onto them.*

Don't: *Read into the 'realistic' things they say, they don't mean offence.*

TO GOSSIP OR
NOT TO GOSSIP

GOSSIP

noun

casual or unconstrained conversation or reports
about other people, typically involving details that
are not confirmed as true.

'She became the subject of much local gossip.'

Right, I'm going to admit it, I have gossiped from
time to time. I'll put my hands up and say that I am
guilty of chatting about friends behind their backs, but
this isn't some kind of grand confession. I don't feel
guilty of a terrible friend-on-friend crime, in fact I think
gossiping can be harmless – and maybe even healthy at
times! Or maybe what I'm describing isn't gossip at all.
Doing research for this section I thought I'd find conflict-
ing views on gossiping, the good vs the bad, but when

looking into gossip and how it affects friendship all I found was a wall of anger and warnings. Everything we read about gossip is negative; we're given tips on how to deal with a gossiping friend and how to avoid becoming friends with one in the first place. According to every article online, gossiping is nothing but bad news. But let's be honest, we all do it! Gossip has a bad rep, one that's maybe worse than the act itself. If it was *so* bad and *so* damaging then why do so many of us still do it and why do we accept it as just part of our female friendships? Maybe because it's not really as bad as we all make out. I think there is a fine line between gossiping and bitching and to me, a harmless gossip is all down to the tone and intention within the chat. It's almost like we need a new word for 'harmless gossip', to differentiate it from the type of bitchy gossip that involves spreading false rumours and talking with a negative tone about someone else.

'Oh my God, did you hear they're breaking up? I knew it wouldn't last long. I bet he cheated on her!' – *Bitchy gossip.*

'Did you hear they're breaking up? I wonder why! I've noticed they haven't been happy for a while and I didn't like the way he treated her. Maybe we should invite her round for cup of tea and see if she wants to chat . . .' – *Harmless gossip.*

'Don't tell her I said this but I just really don't think she's cut out for having a baby. She's clearly so naïve about what to expect!' – *Bitchy gossip.*

'I really hope she gets support when she has a baby as I don't want her to feel overwhelmed, I'm worried she'll struggle . . .' – *Harmless gossip.*

'Did you see her the other night? She was all over the place, it was so embarrassing, LOL!' – *Bitchy gossip.*

'She seemed a bit all over the place the other night, I don't know what's going on but she won't speak to me about it and I'm not sure what to do . . .' – *Harmless gossip.*

So let's talk about this 'harmless gossip' I speak of, as I imagine some of you are reading this, rolling your eyes and thinking *no such thing.* Well, hear me out. If I talk about my friends behind their backs there are a few things I try to consider when doing so . . .

- If I had to, could I say this to their face?
- Am I making anyone around me feel uncomfortable by what I'm saying?
- Do I trust the company I'm in?

As adults, I think we are able to be more aware of each other's feelings and know what is worth confronting and what we just need to get off our chests in a controlled and trusted environment. It's natural for us to chat to friends about how we feel and a harmless gossip is often a way for us to explore and confront our feelings. It's also worth saying that I don't just gossip with anyone who will listen, that's definitely a trait of a *real* gossiper. For me, it's about being with the right person who understands your harmless intentions, otherwise you can get completely misunderstood. Part of knowing the difference between bitching and having a harmless gossip is knowing how you would feel if it were the other way around. I'm sure my friends talk about me and how could I expect them not to if I talk about them? If I were given the option to find out what my friends say about me behind my back I would probably opt not to know because I trust in my judgement on who is a real friend or who isn't. How they choose to manage their emotions and relationship with me when I'm not there is up to them and if it doesn't affect me then it's all good.

I know someone who encountered one of those *real* gossips at work, the kind that just can't help it and probably doesn't even know they're doing it. Manisha was close with her boss Bianca; they had known each other before they started working together so their relationship existed both in the office and out, which was really nice for them both. Manisha knew Jen as she also worked with Bianca but in another team; they weren't close but as they had a work friend in common, it connected them somehow. It was in the office cafeteria one day that Manisha found herself in an uncomfortable situation with Jen; they had started talking about their mutual friend. Out of nowhere Jen started bitching about Bianca, gossiping about why she thought she'd been off work and acting strangely, saying that her head wasn't in the game and she was terribly disorganised; it was a real character assassination that Manisha did *not* feel comfortable with.

The thing is, just to make it worse, Manisha knew the real reason Bianca had been acting strangely: she was going through something awful at home but there was no way she was going to tell this girl who clearly loved a gossip. Jen didn't show any concern or worry for her friend, she simply chose to speculate and spread false rumours. Any good impressions Manisha had of Jen previously were completely diminished; she just thought, *You are not a nice person and I would not like to be friends with you.* It completely changed how she saw Jen as a person and if anyone asked about her, she'd honestly say she didn't get a good vibe and that she had a bad experience with her. She didn't indulge in gossip because she couldn't: sharing the ins and outs of the story would make her a gossip too. Clearly, Jen had no such boundaries. For these types of people gossip works as a sort of currency; they think that by telling you something juicy they're offering you something valuable and it leaves you feeling uncomfortable and as though you've failed for not giving anything in return. It takes some serious confidence to say, 'I don't feel comfortable with this situation.' I know in the past I've wimped out and offered up some low-level, widely known 'gossip' to feel like I've contributed somehow.

My first experience with gossip was in my tween days when I started writing a diary. The things I would write about my friends when they upset me would be really quite spiteful. At the time, I would have been horrified if they'd read it but now we read it together and laugh at the immaturity of it all. But we *all* did it, we all wrote bitchy things about each other in our diaries, and we all survived. It was a relief to be able to get any ugly, negative thoughts out of our heads and onto paper locked up and hidden under our beds. But as adults we can be more rational with our thoughts; the risk as we grow up is sharing those thoughts and learning what is OK to say and what's taking it too far.

In the past, I've got myself into really difficult situations and have had to put my guilty hands up. You know when you type out a bitchy text, press send and then your heart stops, you freeze ... *the worst has happened.* You sent the text to the person you were bitching about. *How has this happened? IN WHAT CRUEL WORLD CAN SOMETHING SO TERRIBLE HAPPEN!? Yep, I've been there.* For a moment you think, how can I save this? Maybe I can text saying, 'Sorry this wasn't meant for you, I was just talking about my *other* friend Jane . . . ' No, she'll never believe it. It's too late, it's over, I see our entire friendship flash before my eyes. 'I'm so sorry, I obviously didn't mean to send this to you. I don't know what else to say other than sorry. I'm an idiot. Please forgive me.' Now it's up to the friend gods to mend. They either hear your bitch and somehow see your side of things and just wish they hadn't had to read about it, or they write you off as a friend and don't see the value of keeping you around (if that's the case it probably would have ended at some point anyway). It's the worst and for any of you who have either done this or had this done to you, I feel you. I've been there, desperately trying to work out if deleting a WhatsApp message deletes it from the universe or just from your phone. It's lessons like this that teach you not to gossip about your friends and, more importantly, not to gossip about your friends on WhatsApp.

But how do you move on from something like this? Can you ever forgive a friend for bitching about you behind your back? If the friendship was barely hanging on by a thread then maybe this is the final straw, an excuse for you both to finally move on. But if the friendship means a lot to you and you trust them enough to be able to confront them, have it out, tell them how it made you feel and then decide how you can move forward from it. No one knows how to be the perfect friend; maybe you can give them another chance – who knows, it might be something you look back on and laugh about one day.

When you know your friends inside out you can get

to know who you can harmlessly gossip with and who you can't. One of my friends has such a similar personality to me that I can say almost anything and she'll never take it the wrong way or get offended. We are both equally laid back and there's never any judgement so I can think out loud without worrying about saying the wrong thing. Whereas I have other friends who aren't so sure of the gossip line and if I speak to them about someone else they get all rigid and nervous, worrying that they're involving themselves in proper gossip. I don't ever want someone else to feel uncomfortable so there are definitely some people who I avoid even a harmless gossip with. I also avoid it for my own sanity because if they get defensive and uncomfortable it makes me feel like I've done something wrong, when I know my intentions weren't sinister.

The ugly side of gossip is insidious, it's mean and it's done with bad intentions. This isn't the type of gossip we should experience amongst friends; it's the bad trait we see in a new friend that puts us off getting any deeper into the relationship. It's the kind that starts with, 'Don't tell anyone I said this but . . . ', the kind that makes you feel uncomfortable to be around. If we meet someone who seems to only be concerned with other people's problems and using them as a hot topic to gossip about, it makes us doubt their loyalty and whether they're someone we want to be friends with. It makes us think, is this how they talk about me behind my back? If someone is making you feel uncomfortable it's OK to say, 'I'd rather not talk about this with you.' It's with these friends you find yourself nodding along but thinking, *Actually this person isn't enjoyable to spend time with and they're not happy within themselves*. The thing with gossip is, amongst friends you trust, the line is pretty clear and no one crosses it; those who do, who say that thing that maybe the others are thinking but won't say, are usually the toxic gossipers. I once knew someone who would project their gossiping nature onto me by saying things like, 'Oh, I know you're thinking it too, you're just too scared to say it,' and it takes maturity and courage to say, 'Actually, I wasn't.' The thing with the *real* gossiper is that you can never really get close to them because you can never truly open up and trust them to respect your privacy and keep your secrets.

SHHH, IT'S
A SECRET!

I'm an open book. I don't know why but I am terrible at keeping my own secrets. Whether it's good news, bad news or something that's just too premature to share, I find myself in the company of a good friend and I'm all theirs, sharing my life away. I'm an over-sharer, I can't help it! Maybe that's why I have such long-standing friendships, because secrets are power-ful things: sharing your own secrets with a friend can really bring you closer together, but at the other end of the scale, keeping secrets from friends can tear you apart. Then there's the responsibility of keeping your friends' secrets, which is the most important. I'm well aware that my openness paired with my occasional harmless gossip makes me seem like the sort of friend who cannot be trusted with a secret, but for me, keep-ing someone else's secret is a different skill to keeping my own. Being loyal to my friends has always been really important to me and I think it's the most integral part of being a good friend and it's something I take very seriously. Keeping a friend's secret is like borrowing something from them and keeping it safe, so exposing a friend's secret means taking ownership of something that isn't yours to take. It's an opportunity to strengthen the bond of a friendship – it's a test!

We know that the more open, honest and raw we are the closer we can become to another person, so keeping secrets can weaken our bonds. Keeping secrets from friends is where it gets complicated; it goes against everything we teach ourselves but sometimes, it can be necessary. Say, for example, your friend is struggling at work and having to fight to keep their job but at the same time you get a promotion and a pay rise. Usually it's something you'd tell her about straight away and you know she'd be happy for you, cracking open the champagne to celebrate. But as a friend you know that keeping the news to yourself and choosing to keep it as a secret for now is the caring and thoughtful thing to do. Being open and honest with every single one of your friends is unrealistic – as we've already discussed, you go to each friend for something different. Maybe you keep a secret from a friend because you think they won't understand, maybe they'll judge you and feel differently about you.

A friend of mine told me a story about her flatmate who had been keeping a secret from her friends for years, until it finally all came out one night over drinks. They'd known each other since they were 14, meeting at school and then going on to university together. Throughout all of those years there were certain feelings and thoughts that she always held back from sharing with friends and the pressure around keeping her secret intensified and became even more complicated. She'd use her different groups of friends so there was always an excuse for not being around or for not making plans and as the groups didn't mix it never seemed unusual. After university, they went their separate ways for a while, using that post-uni time to figure out their future plans, but after a year they reconnected and both made plans to move to a new city and move in together. It was a bit of an on-going joke between friends that she was *always* the one to pipe up with the love life advice even though she'd only ever had a boyfriend for a short time in the first year of uni, and they'd tease her for acting so experienced.

One night over drinks she'd had enough of the teasing and just came out with it: 'Actually I *have* been in a few long relationships, with girls – I'm gay.' The whole group was shocked, not for any reason other than they just had no idea. She'd had boyfriends, always talked about dating men, she was actively on Tinder and most importantly, she'd never shared her female dating experiences with her friends. Throughout uni she'd kept every date and every relationship a secret and it was during that year after uni that she'd experienced her first long-term, serious relationship. She hadn't been ready to share it, not knowing how her friends would react or if it would change things, but that night she reached a point where she couldn't hide that part of herself anymore.

My friend said at first she felt quite shocked, just thinking 'How have I missed this?' and worrying it made her a bad friend for not noticing. After the shock wore off she just felt sympathetic and sad about the fact she'd had to go through multiple break-ups alone and had to keep her true feelings a secret. In her mind, she was gradually putting the pieces of the puzzle together and making sense of things that hadn't made sense before. She'd always been quite a closed book and a private person, but from then on she became so much more content and relaxed, which only strength-ened their friendship. Despite feeling sad for her, her friends understood why she hadn't told them and they didn't use it against her or doubt her loyalty. They now look back on it as a funny memory and it's meant they all know where they stand and how well they can trust each other to be non-judgemental.

If a secret is your own then a good friend can usually forgive you for keeping it. Someone I know kept her boyfriend a secret from her friends, not knowing how they'd feel about the person she'd chosen to be with. Eventually, when she shared what was a rather complicated relationship status, her friends just felt sad for her that she hadn't been able to talk to anybody about it. A good friend won't make it about them; they'll see the reason why you weren't able to open up and will help build your relationship so you can learn to trust them.

But not all secrets have a happy ending and often it can be the secret-keeping that is more painful than the secret itself. Sometimes a secret can get buried so deep and get tangled in such a complex web of lies that you have to think, *If it eventually comes out what will hurt more, the truth or the fact you kept it a secret?*

'I'm not upset that you lied to me, I'm upset that from now on I can't believe you.' – Friedrich Nietzsche

Let's say you found out something that affects a friend of yours; maybe their boyfriend is cheating on them with someone you know or a friend of yours is seriously unwell and keeping it a secret from their family. Technically these secrets are not yours to tell. But in adult female friendships, sometimes we have to make a choice and decide what is more important, keeping a secret or protecting and looking out for someone you care about.

I know someone who would put their hands up and say they messed up and the secrets they kept destroyed their friendship. I'll let her tell you the story . . .

In the spirit of being open and honest, I admit that the following tale of a friendship lost to lies is entirely my fault. The events unfolded because of an immature jealousy of a new relationship that blossomed between two of my (then) best friends. Let's call them Suzy and Amir. I met Suzy at university, we really hit it off. We quickly became inseparable and decided to live together. She was relatively quiet, effortlessly beautiful but troubled in her own unique way. Amir was my best friend, we met at Youth Club when I was 11; he was not so quiet, not so beautiful and in no way troubled.

They were not a likely pair; in fact the only thing they had in common was me. Inevitably, their two worlds came to meet when I invited Amir to come and stay in our university home. We had been friends for ten years and were comfortable and confident in our relationship. He would sleep in my bed, he was friends with all my friends and it was normal for him to be there 99% of the time. At the time of their meeting, Amir and I had only ever been friends and this was the way I suspected it would stay forever.

As Suzy and Amir spent more and more time together, their relationship moved out of the friend zone and into a relationship. At around the same time, I packed up and moved to London where I lived close to Amir. Suddenly, Amir's all-too-familiar messages telling me about the girl he kissed who used too much tongue, or the one-night stand he had fuelled by vodka, were a thing of the past. These were replaced with messages like: 'How often is too often to send flowers to Suzy's workplace?' It felt impossible to keep the closeness with both friends and as time went on my relationship with Suzy deteriorated. She would come to London to visit Amir (rather than me) and our contact became near enough non-existent out of a fear of what I would relay to Amir. The girl-friend trumped the best friend and naturally, the places, events and people that had been 'mine and Amir's' became 'Amir and Suzy's'. I was jealous and Suzy knew it. When the relationship ended, I was unashamedly over the moon; finally I was able to get Amir back as my best friend and selfishly (regardless of their pain), I could not have been happier.

It was only after they broke up that I was able to admit to myself that clearly I had feelings for Amir. He had always been vocal about his belief that we were 'meant to be together in the end' and for the first time, I felt it too. This is something, even to this day, that I have not told Suzy. After working away for a month, Amir returned and we had a smooch, which naturally progressed into a rela-tionship. I stopped replying to Suzy's messages and Amir and I lost touch with her – too ashamed or perhaps too immature to admit the truth. In a world recorded by Facebook and Twitter, the rela-tionship was not to stay under wraps for long and through friends we found out that Suzy was in the know. At this point you would assume that we would have come clean and explained the situation apologetically. Nope. Despite Amir and me eventually ending our relationship, neither one of us have confessed to Suzy nor spoken to her in years. Two embarrassed and guilty people remain . . . with one friend fewer than before.

The secrets I held both during their relationship and throughout ours afterwards made me push away one of my closest friends. This was purely down to embarrassment, immaturity, shame and a severe lack of courage to do the right thing. It still makes me feel guilty thinking about it . . . *lesson learnt!*

I listened to this story with my hands over my mouth, hanging onto every word, and at the end I sighed and said, 'Wow, I'm sorry you had to live through that.' Romantic relationships are not easy at the best of times but when they intertwine with your friendships and cause chaos it only further complicates things. Firstly, I think it's normal that she didn't know how she felt about Amir until she saw him with someone else. I think long-term male–female friendships often go through an uncertain time, trying to figure out if the friendship is totally platonic. Also, if he stopped being a good friend and just relied on her relationship with Suzy, that makes him a bad friend and that should have been confronted. Maybe she should have spoken to him and told him she wasn't happy with how he was treating her. It should have also been Suzy's responsibility, though, as her friend and as his girlfriend, to encourage him to nurture the friendship he'd had for so long. But the jealousy was there for a reason and she had to scratch it to find out if it was real ... did she owe Suzy an explanation? Probably not. But after knowing how it felt when she had been on the other side, I think she knows that Suzy deserved to be told about their relationship. Well, we all live and learn.

... the one you keep on your good side

THE FRENEMY

The frenemy is not your stereotypical friend; they're not really your friend at all. Whether they're a family friend you can't cut ties with or a friend of a friend who you can't offend, the frenemy has a way of getting right under your skin and winding you up in a way no one else can. She'll dish out the insults but sprinkle them with compliments so no one but you notices. You spend so much time complaining about them and focusing on what makes them tick, it's almost become a hobby trying to keep up the false friendship. It's too much hassle to end the 'friendship' so instead you make minimal effort but she still manages to worm her way back into your life when it suits her. Despite your best efforts, without realising it, you find yourself in a back-and-forth WhatsApp conversation giving away all your deepest secrets whilst she fishes for more but gives away nothing in return.

Do: *Keep them at a healthy distance.*

Don't: *Let them affect your other friendships by taking up your time or emotions.*

THROUGH THICK
AND THIN

You can be the most drama-free person and have the perfect life and then all of a sudden everything comes crashing down around you, completely unexpectedly. It's during these challenges in life and the really low points when we truly rely on our friends and can begin to see who's *really* there for us. My best friend experienced this when both of her parents became sick within the same year and I sat down with her recently to chat about how it affected her friendships. Before I talk about *her* experience though, I thought I'd share mine, as the best friend. For me it was the first time, as an adult, when I'd experienced a friend going through something really traumatic. In this type of situation, I think a lot of us feel very unsure of our role as a friend at first; we worry about privacy, about saying the wrong thing and we wish we could hear their thoughts to know how to behave. There's no rule book and if we haven't been through it ourselves we have no experience to fall back on. Often, especially if the relationship is very close, it'll be a shock to the friend too but we know that it's not about us and we have to step up straight away and do the right thing. You might not know enough about the situation but then you also don't want to ask too many questions; it's an awkward position to be in and finding your correct role as a friend can take a little while. I was so worried that I wasn't doing enough, but now, speaking to her, I know that how I acted instinctively was just what she needed. Supporting a friend through grief is not something we are taught or ever prepare for, which is why it's the ultimate friendship test because it's totally up to your genuine and honest reaction as to whether you pass or fail.

She said that it was difficult to manage her friendships during those first few weeks after finding out the news and she didn't know how to tell her friends, how to react or how to show her emotions . . . it was a completely alien situation to her. It was a new feeling, a new version of herself and she said 'Honestly, I didn't really want to know what this new version of me was really like.' She always thought that in a situation like that she'd pick up the phone straight away to call her best friend, but knowing that people were expecting a reaction from her stopped her picking up the phone, as she didn't feel ready to know what that reaction was. You need time to digest the news and sometimes that can mean taking time out and away from everything, including your friendships. She said the friends that stood out during that time were the ones who got in contact but didn't demand any of her time in return.

I am so sorry to hear the news. I just want you to know I love you, I'm here for you in whatever way you need. I don't expect a reply from you but just so you know, I am going to keep messaging to check in on you. When you're ready to talk, I'm always available. Sending so much love to you and the family. Always thinking of you. Love you loads xxxx

She said it helped knowing that people cared for her but that there was no obligation to respond or to give any answers. It became all too difficult when some friends would demand too much of her headspace with too many questions, suffocating concerns and unhelpful, unnecessary opinions. At the time, she felt so emotionally unstable that she couldn't tell them to stop; she'd shy away from confrontation knowing it might tip her over the edge so she just had to let it happen. For her, that year really shone a light on who her true friends were and who left her feeling disappointed. She said a few people surprised her by coming out of the woodwork and exceeding her expectations. A friend from work stepped up as the 'fun friend' and would encourage her to go out for after-work drinks, which became a nice escape for her away from what was going on at home. The work friend really knew her friendship role in the situation; she knew she wasn't closely attached to the family and used her position in a positive way. When talking about the disappointments she says that it didn't consume her. When something really bad happens, you spend all of your time and energy being upset about it, so she spent more time focusing on the friends who *did* step up and didn't let the ones who disappointed her take up any of her headspace. She said, 'It seemed unimportant compared to everything that had happened.' When I asked what her advice would be to the friend trying to support another, she said, 'Take their lead. It's not your grief, so you don't need to own it. Take their direction on how much they need from you and don't speak in clichés; be real and personal, honest and raw.

It may be really hard to find the words to message, you might be nervous or worried, but don't make it about you, just send the message. Don't require a response, give them the time and space they need and be relaxed about the friendship going forward, things won't go back to normal straight away.'

She said eventually as she learnt to deal with the grief she began to build a script in her mind; she said you work out set things to say to people when they ask how you are, you know all the medical terms and it's this 'script' that keeps you from getting too emotional with people you don't feel close enough to. What's great about having real friendships or having a *best* friend is that sometimes with them you can go off script. It's during these moments that you can take off the mask and be real and, yes, you may get emotional but when it's with someone you can trust, it's OK.

I was told a story about a group of friends whose friendship was tested through a really hard time and almost didn't survive. There were ten girls in the group, they'd known each other since school and two of them in particular, Stephanie and Ruth, were absolute *best* friends, proper BFFs. Stephanie was going through a really hard time; her mum's cancer had spread, and at the same time her grandpa was very ill, so she really felt overwhelmed with sadness. Let me just tell you about Stephanie. She's the 'thoughtful friend', the one who always sends flowers and a card to say congratulations or buys you really thoughtful, personalised birthday presents and never forgets an occasion. Ruth was a bit more private and she travelled a lot for work but it never stopped them being close. It was during this period, when Stephanie's emotions were all over the place, understandably, that they had a huge argument. Stephanie felt that Ruth hadn't been supportive or caring enough and she wanted to write her off as a friend. Ruth was completely shocked; she thought, how can she end a lifetime of friendship because 'I took too long to reply to text messages'? But no matter how little these gestures seemed to Ruth, Stephanie's expectations were higher than Ruth had realised, and Ruth's behaviour had disappointed Stephanie and completely broken her heart. Going through such a hard time made Stephanie realise how different they were as people and she didn't want to be a part of the friendship anymore, no matter how irrational that may have seemed.

Ruth broke down to the rest of the group asking for help, to which they all hoped over time Stephanie would come around and forgive her. Ruth sent message after message apologising and begging for her to reconsider but Stephanie didn't back down; Ruth's efforts were never good enough. The group was split; it got to the point where the girls would avoid each other at joint events, their group WhatsApp was noticeably awkward and things were never the same. It's been a bit of time now and the girls can finally be in the same room, they talk and are civil, but no one really knows if they ever discussed what happened. Their friendship was never the same, they went from being best friends to acquaintances. Stephanie's reaction made the rest of her friends more aware of her expectations when it came to friends; she never spoke up but she didn't think she had to, she wanted Ruth to see her cry for help just by looking into her eyes – isn't that what best friends are for? I wonder if there is any hope for them as friends; can a broken BFF heart mend? I'd like to think so, when they're both in a better and happier place.

#AskLP
How did you stay in contact with school friends when you all went off to university? I'm going to uni next year and have three best friends, two of them I've known since we were three years old and

I really want to keep them as friends but we're all off to different parts of the country.

My best friends and I all went to different universities in different parts of the country but we always tried to make an effort to message each other, sometimes at the end of the week asking how their week had gone or before exam period to say good luck. I found that keeping up some kind of regular contact, whether that's FaceTiming, calling, messaging or commenting on each other's social media, helped us stay in touch. We also made the effort to visit each other at our universities, which was actually really fun and it gave us a better insight into where they were living and meant we could meet each other's new friends. If we went home on weekends we would try to coincide and go home at the same time so that we could catch up and also spend time with our families. It's hard, but the few years at uni will go quickly and if you're good enough friends the time apart won't affect your friendship.

THE BFF

If I asked you who was your *best* friend, would you
have an answer? One friend who stands out amongst
the rest as the most trustworthy, loyal, enjoyable,
caring, understanding and comforting? The one who
ticks all the boxes. Some people answer YES straight
away, no questions asked, and others will turn up their
nose at the idea: 'Don't be silly, I have lots of friends I
go to for different things.' It seems that it's a topic that
really divides opinion; those who have a BFF are
insanely passionate about it and those who don't seem
almost bitter at the pressure to single one friend out
from the rest. But the more people I ask the more I
think the BFF doesn't really exist . . . that maybe it was
all just a popularity contest that we left behind in the
school playground. The idea of a *best* friend and the
rating system we use to identify them is quite bizarre

really, so why are we all so obsessed with the BFF and is it really just a myth we've all believed in this whole time? The story usually starts on the first day of school; two girls sit together and one offers to share the contents of her pencil case. They quickly become best friends, matching their outfits, sharing their birthday parties and throughout their tweens, teens and twenties the friendship just gets stronger and stronger. One is never without the other close by and they understand each other on a deeper level that no one else will ever be able to. They become mums together, their children become friends and well, the rest is history. It's the friendship fairy tale that we all dream of!

Doesn't every Thelma need a Louise or every Romy need a Michele? It's these intense, romantic female best friends that have us thinking that's how it's supposed to be, and for a lucky few it's a reality. My literary agent is an example of this; the one true love of her life is her BFF and she'd be the first to admit that. No matter where their lives take them or the physical distance that comes between them they are household names amongst their friends, both old and new. BFFs, always were, always will be and there's no two ways about it. When I asked her if she ever felt threatened by her BFF making new friends she dismissed the idea of it ever being a threat: 'She'd tell them about me straight away and vice versa.' I guess what solidifies a BFF is that not only are they *your* best friend, but you're theirs back. Often within a group of friends you can have multiple girls thinking you're their best friend, that you're their *one*, but then how can they all be *your* one? What I've found is that most people think the idea of a BFF is childish and in fact they see two or three friends as their 'best' but lean on each one for a different thing. When I pushed for an answer, insisting that they had to pick one, then the length of the friendship was used as a benchmark, '. . . because I've known her since I was six.' As women, we can be quite territorial; we like to take ownership of our friendships, attaching a length of time or a status to them. But actually, how *is* the best friend granted such a royal title?

The BFF Checklist

✓ You've known them for a long period of time
✓ You can share your deepest, darkest secrets with zero judgement
✓ When something great happens they're the first one you call

✓ You know what each other is thinking without having to say it
✓ No argument will ever put the friendship at risk, it trumps everything else
✓ You know more about each other than your families do
✓ You can reminisce about old memories but are constantly making new ones too as the friendship always stays relevant

I have a few friends I would count as my best and they do all serve a different purpose in my life. I cringe at the idea of having to pick one over the others, mainly because I feel mean rating them in order of importance, but also because if my number two picked me as her number two I'd be distraught. Doesn't everyone want to be the *best?* For me, one BFF isn't enough, I need that support system and I really do go to all my friends for different situations. I've been known to overuse the term 'best friends' because luckily, I really do have quite a few! But a memory that always sticks out to me and makes me think, *Maybe that's how I define my best*, is one that I've kept to myself over the years. It was three years ago and Rich had just proposed to me. It all came as a massive shock so straight after it happened, we hung out in our flat for a bit and let the idea sink in whilst it was just the two of us who knew. It was a Friday so we had a family dinner planned; Rich had suggested it but we're a close family so it didn't seem strange to have the plans in place, I was none the wiser. We thought we'd keep the news to ourselves, drive over to my parents to tell them and then head to my sister's to share the news face to face. We were in the car driving over, no one knew and *all* I could think about was when and how to tell my friend Hannah; I was desperate. I decided to just call her then and there; she was at work but picked up straight away saying, 'Hello?' in a suspicious voice (it was out of character for me to call her on a Friday afternoon). I told her the news, we screamed down the phone to each other and she burst out crying at her desk. For the last ten minutes of the car journey I felt so happy and it was so special knowing that only she knew, no one else, not even my mum! I really noticed how I had prioritised her during a time that was so important for me and it wasn't the 30 years of friendship, the memories or the advice she gives to me that cemented her BFF status, it was that moment right there.

PS To my other best friends reading, I love you, don't hate me and please can I still be your BFF? Thanks.

We all crave the status of BFF, but with the status come some hefty responsibilities, one of which I am renowned for complaining about . . .

WILL YOU PLAN MY HEN?

Hen Planner:

Hi All!

We're starting to put some plans in place for Laura's hen now, really exciting!

It's going be in London on **Friday night 4th July and Saturday day/night on 5th July**.

We're working towards £150 per person for the whole hen to make it really special for Laura!

As we're starting to book things, we'd like to ask if you could please transfer the first instalment of money as soon as possible. Laura doesn't want to be the only one in the dark, so we're going to keep some of the activities a surprise for everyone.

We'll of course let you know nearer the time a rough itinerary, what sort of things to wear, travel plans etc. but for now this is all we need from you guys!

Thanks so much,

Xxx

Hen Guests:

'Hey, I'll definitely be there for the Friday night but I just need to check that someone can look after my dog on the Saturday because if not then I can only come for two hours at a time, is that OK?'

'Hey, I'm not sure if I'm free because I might have a work trip that weekend but I won't know until nearer the time so is it OK if I just let you know when I know?'

'Hey, thanks for the invite. I can come to the Saturday afternoon between 2–5pm, is that OK?'

'Hey, looking forward to it. Just checking, as I don't drink, whether the £150 includes alcohol and if so, how much, so I can pay less in total?'

'Hey, can't wait! If you need any help let me know, I spoke to Laura recently and she said she REALLY wanted to do an afternoon tea at this place we once went to together so let me know if you want the details. I think she'd love it!'

'Will you plan my hen?' Five words that can both warm my heart and send shivers down my spine at the same time. For those of you who haven't had to suffer through the wedding phase yet, a hen party is a pre-wedding celebration for the bride and her friends. It can be a day celebration, a simple night out, a whole weekend extravaganza or even a trip abroad; the rules are vague, hence the problem. The first time I helped plan a hen party was for my sister, but I was preoccupied with my gap-year travels and just happy enough to be at a legal age to join in, so it was really left up to her friends and my other sister to plan. When it came to it, I had the best time and thought, *I can't wait until I can do this with all of my friends.* Oh, how wrong I was. If you're the bride you're excluded from this pain – for the bride it actually *is* fun and I can vouch for that – but for everyone else it can be quite the relief when it's finally over. *Come on, we all think it.*

In theory it's such a nice idea, to get all your favourite women together to celebrate a new chapter in your life, but the reality is far more complicated. The bride usually (and I use the term 'usually' because really every hen is so different) designates a few friends to be in charge of planning; sometimes within that group will be a Maid of Honour, a BFF if you like. It's during the planning process when the idea that each friend serves a different purpose really comes into view. I've planned a few hens and it's at that first stage, when brainstorming ideas, that it can be the most frustrating.

From the bride's perspective, I found it quite funny, because I knew that there would be certain people who knew me better and some who *thought* they knew me better. I had three friends plan my hen alongside my two sisters; I knew my friends would be more aware of what I enjoy doing now but I knew my sisters would really value being involved and it was some-thing nice for them to get stuck into after having kids. They all got on fine but they definitely didn't all agree on everything. When communicating to me, one friend took the 'Don't worry it's all fine' route trying to shield me from the conflict, another told me my sisters were 'a little difficult to work with' and well, sisters being sisters, they told me all the gory details. I found the whole thing quite amusing but I wasn't surprised about what I was hearing as I knew which characters would play which role within the planning process and they all lived up to their stereotypes. It did surprise me though how strongly each individual felt about knowing me the best and I could sense the competitiveness, but I was reluctant to break anyone's heart by pointing out who knew me better.

The thing with planning a hen party is there is a lot to consider and essentially you become a part-time party planner alongside your already very busy life. But the hardest part by far is that you're grouped together with the other 'best' friends and more often than not, they're not your friends too. Waiting to be asked to plan a hen and then waiting to find out who you're planning it with is like waiting for exam results.

'I would LOVE it if you'd plan my hen?'

'Of course! Who with?'

'Sarah, you know, my *other* Lily . . .'

SHE HAS ANOTHER LILY?! It's at that point, when you get your results, you realise where you stand in the pecking order and all of a sudden, your BFF status is all up in the air. It's almost like the hen party is your way of proving how well you know them and how thoughtful you are as a friend – *it's game on.*

It's up for debate whether hen planning is best in a big or small group and both have pros and cons really. A large group makes decision-making a nightmare, there are too many cooks in the kitchen and no one

genuinely enjoys a monthly hen meeting. But planning a hen with just one other person is intense, *trust
me*. You think you're a moderately calm person who's
good in a confrontational situation until you find
yourself in a full-on screaming argument with someone you barely know about whether people our age
like to drink wine with their meal or a gin and tonic.
Planning a hen with *my* friends would be dreamy
because I know how to handle them, what makes
them tick and how they like to be communicated
with. But when you're suddenly grouped together
with people you barely know, it's like skipping steps
in the friendship game; there's no time to get to know
each other, it's straight to business.

What always strikes me about hen planning is how
each friend really sees the bride in a completely different way and that wasn't something I was prepared
for. When you've known someone for 30 years you
think you know them best, you know *everything* about
them, but then someone else who's also known them
for 30 years can see them in a completely different
light. It makes you question everything and makes
you realise that each friendship is different and you
share a different part of yourself with each friend. It
seems so fickle and now we can look back on it and

laugh, but at the time an argument about whether or not the bride would be embarrassed about having a butler in the buff, or whether she'd take it in her stride and embrace it, really blew my mind. I'd think, *Are we talking about the same person here?!* It makes you doubt how well you really know someone, hence why after the hen there's always the debrief of what we were *going* to do but couldn't, just to cement our intentions and not be judged as a friend by the final result, which may have been compromised.

Once you've battled with the planning process, one of you then gets the lucky job of the 'communicator', the head of all emails, the money-chaser and the customer support. So not only do you have to get on with the *other* best friend but you now have to navigate your way through ten other new personalities.

We spend so much time hand-picking our friends and perfecting our 'friend-edit' that we don't often give much thought to our friends' friends, who *they* choose to surround themselves with, and you can definitely learn a lot about a friend by meeting theirs. A hen is often the first time you'll have all of your different friends and friendship groups in one place and it's a pretty bizarre experience.

10 Types of Hen Personalities

- **The Control Freak** – *she needs to know every detail, has lots of opinions and tries desperately to get involved with the planning.*
- **The Flake** – *she'll seem super keen but then takes ages to reply to emails and drops out last minute with a lame excuse.*
- **The Entertainer** – *she is great to have on a hen, if the mood dips she'll pick it up with a spontaneous game and her high energy level is valued!*
- **The Non-Drinker** –*when the hangovers are bad she's a painful reminder of our former sober selves.*
- **The Flight Risk** – *she's the one who will slip away during dessert, texting the bride 'Sorry I had to go, wasn't feeling well!' thereby messing up numbers for the post-dinner game.*
- **The Loner** – *she doesn't know anyone else so is a bit awkward at first but someone will always take her under their wing eventually.*
- **The Family Member** – *usually a sister-in-law or younger cousin who feels a little out of place and cringes during the risqué games.*
- **The Boozer** – *she's the one who takes it a little too far and has to be put in a cab home. She makes for some great stories though!*
- **The Money Moaner** – *there's always one who needs to know exactly where her money is going and has an opinion on where the budget should be spent.*
- **The Games Grinch** – *she rolls her eyes and opts out of the games because she's just too cool.*

I've learnt from my hen planning days to avoid WhatsApp groups or email chains that include guests and that two or three opinions are more than enough; 20 would be impossible to manage. I think we've all been scarred by the WhatsApp groups we've wished we weren't in. You know, the ones you wish you could leave without 'Lily has left the group' popping up for everyone to see. *Thank God for the mute button.* I know by now which friends of mine will message back straight away, which ones will take days to reply and who prefers a phone call. But a hen group? Well, that's full of a whole load of unknown users. I planned a hen with a girl who, she won't mind me saying, is obsessed with voice notes. Apparently, she's too busy to type so I spent the best part of six months holding my phone up to my ear whilst listening to her share her wandering thoughts whilst parallel parking. I've also experienced the 'yes girl', the one who says OK or agrees with anything you say, thinking she's being easy to work with, but actually is just putting all the decision-making on you instead. Now just to balance things out, let me tell you that I am not guilt-free when it comes to being a cooperative hen planner. I am without a doubt the care-too-much, control-freak friend who wants help and doesn't want to be left alone to plan but also secretly hates everyone else's suggestions. *Yep, that's me.*

Through planning hens I've learnt how to work with new people and personalities I'm not used to and I've learnt that although I may think I know my friend best, every friendship is different and I think we genuinely do show different parts of ourselves to different friends.

#AskLP

I'd be interested to hear your opinion about letting go vs holding on to friendships when you grow apart. Can you still care about someone you don't really like much anymore? I'm experiencing this with someone who I considered my closest friend. Life has made us grow differently, she has drastically changed in the last two years ... and I just don't connect to her anymore. It's sad really.

It's difficult when a friendship just grows apart, without an argument or anything to be angry about, you're right ... it's just sad. Sometimes we take on different paths, grow to enjoy different things and our personalities just don't match up like they used to. If it were me, I would try to decide how important that friendship is to me. Do I love them enough to want to keep them around even if we're not as close as we once were? If so, then maybe it's just about adjusting the friendship and changing your expectations, finding other friends to fill the role they once took. If you no longer want them in your life then try to take a break; maybe one day you can reconnect when your lives have changed again and you might be able to get back on track.

AN ODE TO THE MALE FRIENDSHIP

It didn't feel right to explore the ins and outs of my female friendships without even acknowledging the male friends in my life. Because, as you know, my friend journey started with one of each, a guy and a girl. As much as I love my female friendships, growing up, I was always the girl with a boy as a best friend and I loved it; I think it's what made me a 'tomboy' – a title I was always proud of. With best friends as mums, Jake and I were forced together as babies but it didn't take much convincing – we were inseparable from day one. He was the youngest of three boys and I was the youngest of three girls, our eldest siblings were best friends and so it all made sense! Jake is one and a half years older than me, but we never really noticed an age gap growing up; mentally, I truly believe girls mature quicker and physically, he was always small for his age and I was always tall, so we levelled out. *Sorry Jake, but it's so true.* We'd share baths, swap outfits, play 'mummies and daddies', but our favourite pastime was always dancing. Our families often went on holiday together, we spent one New Year's Eve in Scotland celebrating; a four-year-old me and a five-year-old Jake spent the entire night on the dance floor holding hands, jumping up and down and even doing the occasional twirl.

Our mums always stayed close so, despite being in different school years, we spent a lot of time together outside of school. He'd go to karate lessons and I'd go with him to sit and watch, and when I had girly sleepovers, I'd always invite him to come along too. He got pretty used to always being the only boy and, well, as a natural-born performer, he never minded the attention. Our families were so close, we'd sometimes spend Christmas together and so he was always more like a brother to me.

We stayed close throughout secondary school but obviously the dynamic changed, as it always does, when the complications of teenage emotions arrived. I always hung out with him and his friends playing football or video games but I remember suddenly feeling quite aware that I was the only girl, when it had

never really mattered before. I started dressing differently, in a more girly way; I was leaving my 'tomboy'
days behind me. The boys would make jokes that I
didn't find funny and it just seemed that our interests
were suddenly different and divided. I also remember
the first time Jake showed an interest in one of my
friends, saying he thought she was pretty, and I felt
weird about that, because before he just felt like one of
the girls. I suddenly realised that he was a boy with his
own boy feelings and boy intentions; it divided us in a
way it hadn't before. He started talking about girls
more and caring what they thought and I just had no
interest in that side of him, it was boring to me. The
love between us as friends was so strong though that
no matter what hiccups or awkward teenage phases
we had to live through, we'd always come out the other
side just as strong. Any new boyfriend I had would
have to meet Jake and get his approval; my husband
still remembers when I took him to meet Jake and he
was terrified just knowing our history, but he had
nothing to worry about, like I'd told him.

Jake has always made a huge effort to get on with
my boyfriends and friends, which means that we've
managed to stay close over the years. At 15 he started
dating one of my closest girlfriends, which completely

changed the dynamic again, and it definitely took us a while to find a balance between friend and friend's boyfriend/girlfriend's friend. I'm not really a jealous person so that wasn't ever a problem but I found that Jake got lazy and felt he didn't need to message or call me directly as much; I'm sure I did the same. The friendship between girls is more consistent, so he'd find out updates about me through her and vice versa, so we wouldn't feel the need to speak as often. They were together for ten years but when that relationship ended, we had to find a new rhythm again in our friendship.

The thing with Jake is that we'll never not be friends – it's a fact, we have a bond so strong and a history so deep that it just would never happen – *but* having a male best friend is definitely different to having a female one. Jake and I can go months without talking; he'll vaguely hear what I'm up to through his mum and I'll do the same but our communication is less than ideal. He's a professional opera singer who travels the world and I can barely keep up with what country he's in, but we'll always keep on top of each other's social media platforms, checking in when we can. Even if months pass, when we see each other, nothing has changed. When I got engaged I knew that no one else but Jake could marry us; we played 'weddings' enough times as kids that it only made sense. He led the emotional ceremony making people laugh and cry and later at the party, like we've done for almost 30 years, he spun me around the dance floor. People always teased us saying that one day we'd end up getting married, but honestly, we both always knew our friendship was totally platonic. I hear that all the time: 'Can a friendship with a man ever just be platonic?' It's been almost 30 years since Harry met Sally and declared that a man and a woman could never be friends because 'the sex thing keeps getting in the way', but I'm sorry, Harry, you were wrong. We're living proof that it is possible and the movies lie. Never have we even considered a romantic relationship; the thought makes us both cringe because we're literally like siblings. Being slightly older, Jake has always been more of a protective brother figure; we could hang out together, go clubbing with friends but in the background, he was always looking out for me in some way.

So, what is it about male friendships and why do we still need them if we have our girls? I think they bring a different type of friendship, a somewhat less intense one that can be just as beneficial without all the hard work. I find that if I talk to my male friends about a problem or a worry, they'll reply with a really rational, matter-of-fact suggestion that I wouldn't have thought of. Sometimes I need a girlfriend to be able to go through the emotions but often a male friend will prevent me from getting in a flap.

In my third year at university I moved into a three-bed house with two guys. One of them, Giancarlo, half Brazilian, half Italian, is a real 'loving life' kind of guy; he'd drag me out of the house on a fun night out if I was feeling down or whip up a meal for us all during intense study periods. Our other housemate was Jay, a German guy who I didn't know that well before living together. We definitely had our cultural differences and it took a while for us to become real friends. He was so 'to the point' that sometimes I thought he was being rude, but then I realised that was just how he communicates and it's actually what I really like about him now. He was so brutally honest about absolutely everything, whether I was asking him for his opinion on my blog or if we were work-ing together on a uni project. What you see is what you get, which makes the friendship so easy. Jay made a massive impact on me; he helped me set up my blog in the living room of our house in 2010, which started this entire journey for me. Eight years later and Jay has lived in both Australia and Berlin and we've always kept in touch via Skype, WhatsApp and email. He's continued to be my website developer but also my creative wingman when it comes to most things to do with my work. Living with two men was such a great experience for me; it was simple, it was fun and it showed me the real benefits of male friendships.

As a teenager I enjoyed having male friends mainly because I found them to be so low-maintenance; we never got into arguments or bitched about each other behind each other's backs, but the friendships I have with men have changed throughout my twenties. I've become incredibly close with my friends' boyfriends and husbands, we're now proper friends in our own right and as well as this, it has only strengthened the female friendships and brought us closer as a group. I know that they would all be there for me at the drop of a hat if I needed them, and that we can have a friendship outside of the ones I have with their wives. Although a male friendship can be easier, I think men get a bad rap for being thoughtless, when in fact I think my male friends are quite sensitive and thoughtful; they just reserve it for when they think it really matters and they have to feel really comfortable to be able to open up and share that side to them.

As I write this, Jake is flying back from Italy; he has a few hours at home before leaving for Australia for over a month. *This is how it's going to play out* – I'll text him to say, 'When are you off?' He'll say, 'Tuesday night,' and tell me how manic he's been, and then we'll have a quick catch-up via text on all important life movements. I'll text him before his flight to say 'Safe flight,' stalk his social media for the next month, we might message a few times whilst he's away and then we'll catch up properly when he's home. Now if this was one of my girlfriends it would be completely different; she would have texted me before flying home to say how long she's back for and we'd book in a time to make sure we had a quick catch-up before she left again. I would prob-ably have bought her a good luck card and maybe some in-flight essentials for the journey. She would have texted me when she landed and FaceTimed a few days in, we'd WhatsApp almost daily sending photos and videos so that by the time she came home I'd already know all the details from the trip. *It's just different.*

Our female friendships are just more complex – *fact.*

F IS FOR . . .

Women have lusted after love for long enough. I am over the moon that, now, we seem to be valuing friendship more than ever before. Within my own personal social media bubble, the women I follow seem to be speaking up more in general and sharing their opinions on all kinds of topics. If I scroll through my Instagram feed I see my friends at Coppa Feel posting an abundance of boob-related photos to encourage and empower young women to take charge of their bodies and check their breasts. I see an organisation called 'The Pink Protest' starting a #freeperiods campaign to call on the government to make tampons free to girls already receiving free school meals across the UK. I see my Insta-friend Scarlett Curtis sharing short videos of women speaking up about mental health, using #icontinue as a way to show other women that they're not alone. Then yesterday I saw a friend, who lent a story for this book about how she struggles to trust women and make friends after being let down, post a photo of herself and a friend from work, writing: 'Spending the week with this babe was a real dream. She made me laugh, kept my spirits high and made me do yoga when I didn't want to (it's my least favourite thing)' with the emoji that sums up the joy of most of our female friendships . . . (checks Emojipedia for official name) *women with bunny ears partying'*.

We might not all be screaming from the rooftops about the importance of our female friendships but in some way, it seems to be creeping in as a topic we want to talk about more and more. One of the most popular topics that people comment to me and my friend Anna about online, whether it's under photos or videos, is #friendshipgoals; in fact there are 4,360,362 photos tagged with that on Instagram and with #couplegoals at 5,087,396, the competition isn't far off. But what are friendship goals? That bond you wish you had with someone, a connection unlike any other, a friendship so strong it can survive anything . . .

Urban Dictionary Definition:

Usually two people that are inseparable, tolerate each other's crazy lives, deal with their emotions whether happy or sad, would go to the ends of the earth to make sure their friend is happy, and other people are usually jealous of their unbreakable bond.

Those girls are friendship goals because they can always count on each other no matter what.

When I set out to write this book I thought I had a pretty good idea of all the intricacies within our female friendships and all the challenges and rewards that come with them, but through speaking to others and spending time looking into my own friendships I have learnt so much more than I'd expected. I've always known how much my friends mean to me but until writing down the stories and relating the memories, I hadn't considered all the ways in which they've truly shaped me. It's strange to think of how much I would differ now as a person if I hadn't had all of these experiences to reflect on and learn from. Having a close female friend is like holding a mirror up to yourself; she can expose your worst traits and biggest insecurities but can also bring out the most beautiful version of you. I've learnt that although we spend so much time discussing the right and the wrong types of friends, often when we look at ourselves we can discover the root of our complications. Could it be our own insecurities and fears causing us to hold back from a true and honest friendship? Our friends can show us a different side to ourselves we hadn't noticed before, but it's because of this that we are able to grow and constantly work on becoming better people.

We start out in the world of friendship hunting down that one best friend but really what I've realised is that most of us don't have just one best friend, we have a collection of friends for all different scenarios. It's within our friend 'edit' that we try to create a balance; no matter how great you might be at being the 'older sister' friend, everyone needs someone to lean on for support. Your friendships should give back as much as they take; remember it's all about keeping those weighing scales balanced out. It's not always obvious when you first meet someone what role they could take on as a friend, but you find your natural rhythm together and even then, it will change over time. The role we take on as a friend is circumstantial and as we grow and navigate through life, it's constantly changing and adapting and I think it's what's key to a healthy friendship. When Hannah was getting married she felt overwhelmed and completely out of her comfort zone and so we switched and I stepped in to take on the temporary role as the 'older sister friend' because when your friends really need it, you're there for them even if that means stepping outside of your own comfort zone. I feel very lucky to be surrounded by so many incredible female friends, but if you read this and struggle to make or hold onto them then I hope it's inspired you not to give up. There are always new opportunities to make friends; there's always potential to find that one person you can totally be yourself with. Sometimes it's hard to become close friends, sometimes it's as easy as slipping on the perfect pair of shoes, but what it comes down to is always keeping an open mind to new opportunities. Even if you think you're just not a 'girl's girl', destined to have only male friends, there's always going to be *someone* who feels the same, who you just click with.

I hope this book has made you hold a magnifying

glass up to your friendships and see them for what they really are. I hope it's made you appreciate the beauty and complexity of the bonds you hold with the women around you, because really, they should be celebrated. Our life is made up of so many people, partners, family, colleagues, but the female friends who you choose to surround yourself with, your 'tribe' if you like, become your safety blanket. Your girl squad, your besties, your BFFs, they're the ones who make you *you*.

On Christmas Eve, my best friend took a one-way flight to Australia.

Our spontaneous tea chats are no longer a thing and early morning scheduled FaceTime appointments have taken their place instead, but despite my inability to talk about it without crying, I'm trying my best to embrace her exciting new journey. Because maintaining female friendships is about adapting, being flexible and putting in the work, and even if that means keeping a list of things you want to tell her for the next time you speak or filming moments you don't want her to miss to send to her when she wakes up, it's worth the time and effort, because there's no way anyone else could fill the hole that she'd leave if the friendship ended.

Female friendships – they're never straightforward. But no matter the struggles we feel at times, no matter the let-downs and strife in our relationships with other women . . . it seems the reward is *always* far greater in the end and I personally wouldn't have it any other way.

ACKNOWLEDGEMENTS

Firstly, I'd like to thank my family and my husband Rich for always supporting and encouraging me, especially all those years ago when I packed in my job to pursue an unknown career. Rich, thanks for putting up with me during this project and for always celebrating every little success with me.

Thank you to Briony Gowlett for giving me the opportunity to explore a subject close to both of our hearts. I felt that 'new friend spark' in the very first meeting and it's been such a pleasure working with you since.

A big thanks to Abigail Bergstrom for getting me started with this huge new project, I don't think I ever would have got through it without you and it was so encouraging knowing you share the same passion for the topic as I do.

To my wonderful management team at Gleam Futures; Lucy, Georgia and Millie who have become incredible friends of mine. Thanks for always being so patient and understanding, and for letting me cry on the sofa in your reception area (sorry about that!).

To my girls, some of whom I've known for over 27 years, who have shaped my life and who have created this book without even realising it. Hannah, Debs, Gemma, SJ, Keisha, Jenny, and of course, Jake (he's one of the girls really), I wouldn't be without you. A special thanks to Hannah for reading this entire book on a flight to Shanghai. I just needed to get that 'older sister friend' approval.

Thank you to my work wife Anna for letting me rant on the phone, for always being free for a brainstorm and for having so much faith in my abilities. We've been on this crazy journey together almost since day one and I love that even our separate projects feel like joint ones.

And finally, to all my Internet friends; the hundreds of thousands of women all over the world who watch my videos and engage across all of my platforms. I've somehow managed to build a tight community of incredibly kind, intellectual and passionate women who constantly push me to do better, create more and enjoy celebrating being a woman. Whether you've watched me from the start, or only just discovered my content, thank you for caring about what I've got to say . . . I really do appreciate it every day.

ABOUT THE AUTHOR

Lily Pebbles is a UK blogger and vlogger who shares her beauty, fashion and lifestyle content across multiple social platforms online. She started her blog in 2010 whilst studying marketing, advertising and public relations at university and later went on to create her YouTube channel in 2012. What started as a university project went on to become a passionate hobby and in 2013 she quit her job as a marketing manager to try blogging and vlogging full-time.

Since then her audience have grown with her as she's moved homes, got married, travelled the world, launched a chart-topping podcast and collaborated with global beauty and lifestyle brands.

'I'm so grateful that my job started off as a hobby, because the organic growth my channels have seen over the past eight years has created a really kind,

supportive community full of amazing, powerful women (and a few men too!). Being honest and authentic online has always been incredibly important to me and this book was a chance for me to open up even further about a topic that's so close to my heart. My goal is to encourage both my viewers and those who have never followed me online, to celebrate their female friendships because personally, I would be nowhere without mine.'

I really hope you enjoyed reading this book and thank you so much for taking the time to do so.

Come and join our lovely online community . . .

  @lilypebbles

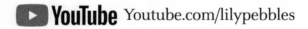 Youtube.com/lilypebbles

www.lilypebbles.co.uk